From Day One

From Day One

Why Supporting Girls Aged 0 to 10 is Critical to Change Africa's Path

By Joyce Banda
With Caroline Lambert

CENTER FOR GLOBAL DEVELOPMENT
Washington, D.C.

Library of Congress Cataloging-in-Publication Data

Names: Banda, Joyce, 1950- author. | Lambert, Caroline, 1970- author.
Title: From day one : why supporting girls aged 0 to 10 is critical to change
    Africa's path / by Joyce Banda ; with Caroline Lambert.
Description: Washington, DC : Center for Global Development, [2018]
Identifiers: LCCN 2018012355 (print) | LCCN 2018021154 (ebook) |
    ISBN 9781944691080 | ISBN 9781944691073 (pbk. : alk. paper)
Subjects: LCSH: Girls—Africa—Social conditions. | Girls—Africa—Economic
    conditions. | Sex discrimination against women—Africa.
Classification: LCC HQ777 (ebook) | LCC HQ777 .B243 2018 (print) |
    DDC 305.23082/096—dc23
LC record available at https://lccn.loc.gov/2018012355

Contents

Preface

This book was written to fill a gap. Grounded in research and practical experience, it makes the case that Africa cannot fulfill its potential unless its rural girls aged 0–10 are given a better chance.

The case for gender equality is well established: providing equal opportunities, voice, and treatment to women and girls benefits not only individuals, but entire economies. The impact echoes across generations, as healthier and better-educated mothers improve life chances for their children. Women in leadership positions are not only role models, but they also have been shown to influence policy priorities and business practices and to make a positive contribution to conflict resolution and governance. Yet gender policy has so far largely focused on women and adolescent girls, while interventions focusing on children are typically not gender specific. As a result, pre-adolescent girls have received little attention.

Until now.

These pages make the case that gender discrimination, particularly in rural areas, does not start at adolescence: by the time African girls turn 10, their minds and bodies have already been shaped in ways that bear consequences for the rest of their lives, stunting their leadership potential or even silencing it entirely. Looking at nutrition, labor and household chores, harmful traditions, as well as education, the author offers recommendations not only for governments and donors but also for civil society and individuals in Africa and elsewhere.

Joyce Banda has produced a compelling and accessible narrative, weaving personal stories with research. She brings her unique perspective and a wealth of experience to the field of gender policy. Her positions are informed not only by her own experience growing up in the continent but also by her tireless activism to support girls and women, as well as her extensive government experience. A lifelong activist and Malawi's first female president, Joyce Banda is an inspiring role model for girls in Africa and beyond.

It has been CGD's honor to welcome Joyce Banda as a visiting fellow and to support her research about young African girls. Her work resulted first in an essay—*An Agenda for Harmful Cultural Practices and Girls' Empowerment*—which then provided the foundation for these pages. She has greatly contributed to CGD's gender work. It is my hope that this book, by shedding light on an area that has so far received little attention, sparks debate, advances gender interventions, and further levels the playing field for all African girls and women.

Masood Ahmed
President
Center for Global Development

Acknowledgments

I have been blessed with the support of many people in the making of this book.

These pages would not have been written without the generous support of the Brenthurst Foundation. I particularly wish to thank Greg Mills, the foundation's director, and President Obasanjo of its advisory board.

By offering me a visiting fellowship, the Center for Global Development (CGD) has supported the research that first turned into an essay and eventually inspired this book. Special thanks to Todd Moss for making it happen; to Priscilla Atansah for co-writing that first essay and providing administrative support; to Rajesh Mirchandani and Emily Schabacker for managing the publication process; and to Tanvi Jaluka and Gailyn Portelance for their assistance with research.

Thank you to Masood Ahmed and Charles Kenny of the Center for Global Development, as well as Megan O'Donnell of ONE and Markus Goldstein of the World Bank, for providing insightful comments on the first draft.

Before meeting Caroline Lambert, my co-author, I had no clue about how to write a book. She made it easy, skillfully translating my vision onto the page. She weaved my thoughts and my stories, and strengthened my arguments through her own research, insights, and narrative sense. Our collaboration, fueled by common purpose, tea, and good conversations, has been an absolute joy.

I would not have written this book without the encouragement of my husband, Richard Banda, who for over 35 years has been an unwavering source of love and support through thick and thin.

I owe much to my late father, Gray Mtila, who believed in his daughters from day one, and to my late mother, Edith, who stood by him, no matter what.

Joyce Banda

Introduction

"This child is going to be a leader."

This is what a friend of my father said when I was eight years old. As I grew older, my father never let me forget it. "Remember what Uncle John said," he kept telling me. "You are destined to be a leader." I didn't know a leader of what, but I came to believe that in every situation, I had an opportunity to do something, to lead and to make a difference. I was lucky to have a father who believed in his daughters' potential.

I also understood at a young age that the vast majority of girls were not so lucky. In my village of Malemia in Malawi's Zomba district, my best friend was Chrissie. Both Chrissie and I were born in that village. I come from a matriarchal tradition, and as the firstborn girl in my family, I was supposed to be brought up by my mother's mother. Yet my father wanted to bring me up and send me to school in town. A compromise was struck: I would spend the week in Zomba town with my parents, and every Friday from the time I was seven years old, I took the bus to travel the 15 kilometers to Malemia, where I would stay with my grandmother. And every Friday without fail, Chrissie would wait for me by the roadside, and we would walk into the village together. Chrissie taught me all about village life. We picked wild fruits and wild mushrooms, and we fished for crabs. She taught me how to swim in the village river. She also taught me how to carry heavy loads and work hard at household chores from a very young age—a valued quality in village girls, and an essential part of our upbringing.

Chrissie was better than I was at everything. She was better at carrying heavy loads, and she was better at school. She was at the top of her class. I was not. Yet I became a civil servant and a businesswoman. I also became an activist for women, youth, and children. I became a member of Parliament, and then a government minister. Later, I became vice president and then president of Malawi. And Chrissie? Chrissie never left Malemia. She had to drop out of school, and I kept going. She stopped talking to me. She married and had a child while still a teenager. To this day she can still be found in the village, cooking over a fire. For a long time, her silent question cast a very dark shadow over our friendship. "Why? Why you, and not me?"

Even as a young girl, I asked myself the same question. Why Chrissie? How many are there like her? And what can I do? I decided there and then that this would be my life's purpose. This would be my fight. So I grew up and I took this on as a businesswoman, helping other women become financially independent. I took this on in Parliament and then in government. I took this on in State House when I became president. I'm still taking this on through the Joyce Banda Foundation. And I will keep at it until the job is done.

Chrissie's story is a tragedy. A tragedy of unfulfilled potential. A tragedy for Chrissie herself, but also a tragedy for Malawi and for Africa. In fact, it is a global tragedy: over 130 million girls around the world are not in school through no fault of their own.[1] Girls and women are one of our continent's most valuable assets. Yet there are still many Chrissies: bright, ambitious village girls full of potential, ready to become the kind of leaders that Africa needs so badly and will not get. All because that potential is not given a chance to thrive.

If we want to change Africa's narrative, we need women leaders. A lot of women leaders. Why? First, women make up half of all Africans, and it is common sense that they should be sitting at the table and participating in leadership. Having more women in leadership roles has been shown to have a positive effect on policy decisions,[2] as female leaders focus more on issues that impact women, as well as on corruption.[3] A recent survey in five countries—Kenya, Senegal, India, Colombia, and Indonesia—confirmed that over two-thirds of women policymakers thought that gender equality was getting too little attention in their country, an opinion shared by only one-third of their male counterparts.[4] The moment Ellen Johnson Sirleaf was elected as Liberia's president in 2005, she supported the creation of a market women's fund. Throughout my time in office, I worked hard to narrow the gender gap.

There is no shortage of evidence that when women and girls are given the same education, health, and economic opportunities, and an equal voice in society, the whole country benefits. This is why achieving gender equality and empowering all women and girls is part of the United Nations' Sustainable Development Goals. A growing body of research has confirmed that closing the gender gap improves economic growth and competitiveness.[5] A World Bank report found that eliminating gender inequalities in education and access to farming inputs in Kenya, for instance, could boost economic growth by 4.3 percentage points to start with, followed by consistent annual increases of 2–3.5 percentage points.[6] Rwanda—one of the fastest growing economies in Africa—has a higher proportion of women in Parliament than any other country in the world: 64 percent of MPs in Rwanda's lower house are women, well ahead of the 32 percent in the United Kingdom or 19 percent in the United States.[7] When President Kagame is asked why he has championed gender equality, his answer is simple: "It is logic and common sense. Women are as talented and as skilled as men. . . . When you sideline them, you lose something big."[8]

Besides fostering economic and social development, I believe women leaders are better able to prevent and resolve conflicts. Most of the conflicts on the continent—or anywhere—are not caused by women. And whenever there is conflict, peace agreements have a better chance to be concluded and to last when women are involved in the negotiations.[9] When I was president, for instance, I asked the former presidents in Southern Africa to mediate the border dispute between Tanzania and Malawi. At the same time, I had lawyers write an opinion about our border that would allow us to take the matter to court, if necessary. I also joked with President Kikwete of Tanzania that if he was looking for somebody to fight with, it would not be me, and we successfully partnered to avoid conflict. This is not weakness; this is conflict prevention—and common sense. Ellen Johnson Sirleaf demonstrated that she could turn around a country ravaged by civil war. Catherine Samba-Panza successfully eased the sectarian killings that devastated the Central African Republic when she was interim president from 2014 to 2016.

Africa has a long tradition of female leaders, particularly before colonization, with examples such as Candace de Meroe in the Kingdom of Kush (Ethiopia) and Queen Mother Yaa Asantewaa in what is now Ghana.[10] Independence and liberation movements also owe much to women such as Rose Chibambo, Joice Mujuru, Winnie Mandela, and Albertina Sisulu. Some regions in countries such as Malawi and Ghana maintain matrilineal or matriarchal traditions like my own. Over the past 20 years, there has been progress in political representation: women accounted for 23 percent of MPs in sub-Saharan Africa in 2017, compared to 10 percent in 1997. This places the region at the global average.[11] Yet these numbers still fall short. Only four countries in sub-Saharan Africa have had women heads of state in recent history: Liberia, Malawi, the Central African Republic, and Mauritius. And even in Rwanda, women's stellar representation in politics has not yet translated into more equality at home[12] or significant practical gains for the majority of women in the country, particularly in rural areas.[13]

Most of the many African girls who are born leaders face too many obstacles to realize their potential as change makers. Those who live in villages are often locked in a vicious cycle of poverty, abuse, and harmful traditions. In sub-Saharan Africa, 60 percent of girls live in rural areas; in some countries, including my own, but also Burundi, Uganda, and Niger, the proportion is over 80 percent. If we are going to achieve the Sustainable Development Goals, we cannot leave them behind.

Programs seeking to empower women in sub-Saharan Africa—from microcredit, entrepreneurship, and education to gender-specific cash transfers and social assistance—have multiplied. Many of these interventions now target girls. Let Girls Learn, the multi-agency initiative launched by President Obama and First Lady Michelle Obama in March 2015, focuses on adolescent girls. So did a similar initiative fostered by the Bush administration. In 2016, the World Bank pledged that it would invest $2.5 billion over five years in education projects that directly benefit girls aged 12–17.[14] UNICEF, the UN agency supporting children, has included adolescent girls in its gender strategy. Initiatives such as the Coalition for Adolescent Girls, launched in 2005, seek to address a "girl gap," pointing out that developmental assistance has focused on either women or young children.[15]

Interventions focused on women and adolescent girls are critical to closing the gender gap and fostering female leaders. These efforts are essential to the future of Africa.

Yet a critical piece is missing: interventions supporting rural girls from 0 to 10 years old. Gender interventions tend to focus on women and adolescent girls, while programs targeting young children are typically not gender specific. This leaves out girls aged 0–10. Unfortunately, discrimination and social norms that penalize girls and women do not start at adolescence. By the time many rural girls are 10, it is often too late to undo the damage that has already been done. As an African woman leader who has grown up on African soil, I have seen firsthand how young rural girls face obstacles in areas that are critical in shaping their future as they grow into adolescents and women.

What are these critical areas? We need to take a good look at nutrition, household work, sexual violence, harmful traditions, and education. Some disadvantage young girls more clearly than others, but they all deserve to be examined closely. Nutrition affects the ability to learn and is also crucial to fighting off diseases. Young rural girls work much harder than boys at household chores and caregiving, which not only leaves little time for education or play but also has lasting consequences on their physical development. Unfortunately, many village girls between 0 and 10 years old suffer sexual violence and the impact of harmful traditions. Child marriage and female genital mutilation have rightfully been receiving attention, but there are many other practices with similarly devastating effects that remain unspoken and ignored. And although much progress has been made in closing the gender gap in primary education, enrollment data fail to tell the whole story. In addition, many of the seeds of the inequality that persists at the secondary level are planted well before girls reach high school.

None of these critical areas can or should be tackled in isolation. Change requires more data and evidence, new laws, and the willingness and ability to enforce them, as well as a shift in mentalities and traditions. Change is also a spiraling loop and relies on more girls and women gaining equal education and economic opportunities, and access to leadership and voice—which is why the efforts deployed to support adolescent girls and women are essential. But if we all come together—men and women, governments and civil society, Africans and non-Africans—these obstacles are not insurmountable.

Although women and girls face an uneven playing field at all ages, the challenges they confront in the first 10 years of their lives are not as well understood or perhaps even as visible. But they are nonetheless devastating and must be tackled as well, for much of the future of young girls is shaped during these critical years.

So let us all do our part. Because every girl deserves a chance from the time she is born.

Part I

Challenges for Girls Aged 0–10

1

Nutrition

In most villages in Malawi, there is a place called the *mphala*. This is where men gather in the shade to sit and discuss issues of the village, listen to the radio—often the only radio set in the village—or play games. This is also where they eat. From the time they are five or six years old, boys go sit at the *mphala* and eat with the men. Girls, on the other hand, do not go and sit there. Instead, they stay with their mothers, who fetch wood and water and prepare meals. It is the village wife's duty to cook the best possible dish for her husband and sons and to bring it to them at the *mphala*. It is a matter of pride. It is a matter of tradition. Women compete: who will bring the bigger dish, who will bring the best food? If there are eggs or some chicken, the men and boys eat them. Women and girls get to eat whatever food has not been served at the *mphala*.

So what happens? Whenever there is not enough food for everybody, or not enough meat or vegetables, the boy child has first pick. And the girl? The girl child eats less protein—if any at all—and less food. The girl does not get to hear the discussions about her own community or listen to the radio. Instead, she burns precious calories fetching water or carrying fire-wood. And her mother, after spending the morning tending the garden, pounding the maize, and cooking food, goes to the field again: in some traditions, she has to cut grass to thatch the family roof so it does not leak during the rainy season. She takes her daughter with her, so the young girl learns as young as possible how to do all this work.

So it is in most African villages: men eat first, best, and most. Women and girls eat last and least.[1] Even in my own matriarchal tradition, where women own the land and houses, the situation is not much different when it comes to meals. That mind-set is rooted so deep that it can sometimes be found in urban areas as well. When I was already foreign minister and lived in town, my husband and I were having breakfast at home one morning. He was served one egg, but there was no egg for me.

"Where is my egg?" I asked our domestic helper.

"We have only two eggs left in the house, and I won't do the shopping until tomorrow afternoon," he said. "I'm keeping the other egg for the boss's breakfast tomorrow morning."

"How did you decide who should have the one egg?!" I asked.

No matter how I said it, the idea that food could be evenly shared, or that I might eat that egg instead of my husband, made no sense at all to him. He, as well as others who worked in our house over the years and made the same decision, could not understand what the fuss was all about. Men are supposed to eat first, best, and most. And that was that.

This food discrimination, which is so prevalent in rural areas, results in chronic undernutrition and ill health for village women and girls.[2] Though this unequal treatment continues as girls age, eating the right kind of food and in the right amount is particularly crucial early in life, for it carries lifelong benefits. Babies and young children deprived of essential nutrients such as vitamin A and zinc die more easily, their immune systems unable to fight diseases properly: undernutrition is thought to be responsible for 45 percent of all child deaths in the world every year.[3] Those who survive remain too short for their age—stunted—or too thin for their height, known as wasting. Poor nutrition does not affect size alone, however. When young children are undernourished or malnourished, their brains do not develop as well, which impedes learning as they grow older. And older children who still go hungry struggle to focus in the classroom.

African children are the most malnourished and undernourished in the world. About 57 million children south of the Sahara are stunted—more than a third of the world's total—and 13 million suffer from wasting.[4] There has been significant progress: stunting now affects 34 percent of sub-Saharan African children, down from 49 percent in 1990.[5] At the same time, because population increased faster, the number of African children too short for their age increased by 11.6 million. Besides the human tragedy, under-nutrition costs sub-Saharan Africa up to 11 percent of GDP each year.[6]

In spite of all these numbers, the nutritional plight of rural girls from 0 to 10 in sub-Saharan Africa is not well measured, particularly after 5 years old. The traditions and customs I described earlier are easy to observe and well documented, but very little data and evidence are available beyond country averages and aggregated figures for all children.[7] The few numbers disaggregating boys and girls are not only outdated and patchy, at least in sub-Saharan Africa, but also do not extend to the age when boys and girls start eating separately. For children under five years old, the few disaggregated numbers available suggest no significant gender difference when looking at breastfeeding as well as stunting and wasting. On average, 22 percent of girls are underweight compared to 23 percent of boys.[8] Sometimes, however, comparable stunting between boys and girls is not the result of equivalent nutrition, but rather of the fact that more girls die of malnutrition than boys.[9,10]

In addition, national and regional averages mask differences at the sub-national level. There is some evidence that village children in sub-Saharan Africa eat less than those living in towns: 24 percent are underweight, compared to 17 percent in urban areas.[11] That gap widens dramatically in countries such as Burundi, Eritrea, Ethiopia, Somalia, Burkina Faso, and Niger, where over 40 percent of rural children are underweight, compared to fewer than 30 percent in urban areas.[12]

As for the situation of rural girls older than five, no nutrition data whatsoever appear to be available, at least until they reach adolescence and childbearing age. Yet five or six is the age when rural boys typically start eating with the men, and discrimination becomes visible. Measures focus on children under five years old because this is when the impact of malnutrition is the most devastating and long-lasting. Interventions to improve nutrition have focused on the 1,000 days that span a mother's pregnancy and her child's second birthday, because this is the time window during which much of one's future physical and cognitive development is decided. Once that 1,000-day window has closed, the effects of malnutrition become largely irreversible. Yet malnutrition still carries a heavy price when suffered after five years old, the age when rural girls are most likely to start eating differently from boys.

So although food discrimination affects rural girls older than five—when boys start eating with men—evidence is scant. The impact, however, piles up on rural girls and spills over into the next generation. Girls who are born small and do not catch up, perhaps because their own mothers are themselves malnourished, develop smaller uteruses and ovaries, which in turn results in lower birth weights for their offspring.[13]

Malnourished girls are less likely to go to school, and if they do, they tend to start school late and are more likely to drop out.[14] This puts at risk these girls' own future, but also the prospects of their future children: malnutrition and child mortality decline as mothers' education rises. In Mozambique, for instance, mothers who have received little or no schooling are far more likely to have malnourished children and to use clinics and other health services less.[15]

Why do young rural girls suffer from malnutrition? This is in part due to poverty, which limits families' ability to grow or buy food. Indeed, the proportion of underweight children in the poorest families is almost twice as high as in the richest households.[16] Yet income is not the only determinant: in Malawi, for instance, 53 percent of children under five are stunted—higher than in many African countries with comparable levels of income per capita.[17] Infectious diseases, poor sanitation and hygiene, as well as food and financial crises, conflicts, and natural disasters, all contribute to malnutrition in the region.[18]

Traditional customs and lack of education also contribute to malnutrition generally, and to food discrimination against women and girls in particular. Besides eating less than their husbands and sons, traditions also demand that women and girls refrain from eating certain foods when expecting babies. In parts of Malawi, for instance, pregnant women are not supposed to eat eggs, and they are not supposed to eat okra. Eggs are a good source of protein, and often the easiest to procure in villages. These traditions can further deprive women and girls of the iron, folic acid, and protein they badly need before and during their pregnancy, which undermines their future children's health: undernourished mothers are at risk of carrying smaller babies, which in turn increases the risk of death at birth and stunting by age two.[19]

Poor nutrition knowledge is also at fault. A lack of food variety also compromises nutrition. In most of rural Africa, one single staple food dominates—whether it is maize, rice, or fufu made of cassava. Parts of Malawi, for instance, survive almost exclusively on cassava—the root, but also the leaves. People in those regions eat very little else, and many are stunted as a result.

Better knowledge and a more equitable sharing of food, however, will not improve nutrition unless food production also improves, so that there is enough to eat. In agriculture, as in other areas, a persistent gender gap contributes to the problem. In sub-Saharan Africa, the responsibility of growing and preparing food falls largely on women and girls, while men tend to focus more often on cash crops. On average, women account for about half of all people actively farming, or as high as two-thirds in countries such as Mozambique or Lesotho.[20] Yet women farmers in sub-Saharan Africa produce less than their male counterparts—ranging between 13 percent less in Uganda and 25 percent in Malawi—reflecting a lower productivity per hectare.[21]

Why? Because African women are less likely than men to own land or livestock; to have access to labor, credit, seeds, and fertilizer; to adopt new technology; or to receive education and extension services. In sub-Saharan Africa, only 15 percent of agricultural holders are women, but this average masks wide variations. In some parts of Africa, customary law dictates that women must obtain their husband's authorization to acquire land titles.[22] In the Democratic Republic of Congo, for instance, women make up almost half of those economically active in agriculture, yet less than 9 percent of holders of farmland are women. In Mali, 38 percent of farmers are women, but they account for only 3 percent of landowners.[23] And although over 30 percent of landowners are women in countries such as Botswana, Lesotho, and Malawi, this proportion still falls far shorter of their share in the farming population, which is well above half. Besides the ownership gap, African women are also less likely to have access to rented land. In addition, the plots they farm are often smaller. Inequality in livestock holdings appears to be particularly acute in Ghana and Nigeria, where men own three times more livestock than women who head their households. Even in my own matriarchal tradition, in which women own land, access to land is a problem, as plots get divided among many daughters and become ever smaller.

Women also face greater labor constraints, whether they work their plots themselves or hire extra help. Because of their other domestic responsibilities, such as child-rearing or collecting firewood and water, women typically have less time to farm than men. Poor nutrition, education, and health also weigh on their productivity. In addition, households headed by women typically have fewer family members able to either work on their plots or help at home. They also face obstacles hiring and managing outside help effectively, in part due to cultural norms.[24]

As a result of having less land, time, and poorer access to inputs, labor, and services, women produce less.[25] The FAO estimates that, if these gender gaps were corrected, women could increase yields on their farms by 20–30 percent, which would boost total agricultural output in developing countries by 2.5–4 percent. This additional food production could reduce the number of hungry people in the world by 12–17 percent—or 100–150 million people. For countries where hunger is more widespread and women play a major role in the agriculture sector, as in sub-Saharan Africa, the results would be even greater.[26] If women farmers had the same access to fertilizers and other inputs, maize yields would increase by 11 to 16 percent in Malawi and by 17 percent in Ghana, for instance.[27] In Burkina Faso, reallocating fertilizer and labor more equally between men and women would raise household agricultural production by about 6 percent.[28]

Besides affecting food production, the persisting gender gap also weighs on the nutrition of young rural girls in other ways. Women who have more influence over economic decisions in their own families consistently spend a larger share of income on children's nutrition, food, education, and health. In other words, children eat better, and as a result are healthier and do better in school when women have more bargaining power. In rural Malawi, the nutrition of young children, particularly girls, improved when women had better control over their family resources; the same did not happen when men did.[29]

So, as the UN Food and Agriculture Organization puts it, "the face of malnutrition is female."[30] For the rural girl child in Africa, it often starts in her mother's womb, and if she survives, food discrimination is likely to get worse for her by the time she is five or six years old, with consequences that will echo past her own life and into the next generation.

Yet this is only one of the challenges she faces before she even turns 10 years old.

2

The Burden of Work

In 1995, I needed to undergo surgery. I agreed with my surgeon in Malawi, Dr. Chiphangwi, that he would perform an epidural, which required an injection in the spinal cord, rather than a general anesthesia. Yet when the time for the surgery came, I felt myself losing consciousness. When the doctor came for his round the next day, I was unhappy.

"That was not our agreement," I told him. "You said that you were not going to put me to sleep, but you did."

"You don't know?" he replied. "I couldn't give you an epidural. Your lower spine is bent. Did you carry heavy loads as a young girl?"

Years later, I consulted another doctor about severe hip pain. It turns out the pain was not coming from my hip, but from my lower spine: the doctor confirmed what Dr. Chiphangwi had told me. My spine was badly deformed. Years of carrying heavy loads as a young girl, starting when I was only five years old, had injured my back. In my grandmother's village, it was my friend Chrissie who had taught me to carry water, firewood, or heavy baskets of maize meal on my head. Even in Zomba, there was no running water in my parents' home, and cooking required firewood. I used to wake up at three or four o'clock in the morning to go to Zomba mountain with my friends and collect firewood.

When my mother started working as a shopkeeper to supplement my father's income, I had to look after my three, and then four younger siblings. At age seven, I was already a little mother, carrying babies on my back and feeding them, while taking care of chores at home. Then, when I was 11, my mother had to stay in the hospital for almost a year, and I was in charge of running our home. I never played; there was no time. I was not given a chance to be a child. As the eldest, I was known as "sister." No one called me by my first name. Even today, being addressed as Joyce feels strange and foreign to me.

This is the story of millions of African girls, particularly in rural areas. When I see young girls no older than five carrying heavy loads on their heads with a baby strapped to their backs, I see myself. In most African markets or on roadsides, six- or seven-year-old girls can be found on school days selling bananas or mangoes that they have carried on their heads or on their backs. I wonder how many will live the rest of their lives with an injured spine that can never be repaired. This is a question that, for lack of data, I am so far not able to answer.

In rural Africa, hard work and no play are part of a young girl's training, along with being obedient and quiet. It reflects well on her family. People used to praise my mother for bringing up such a hardworking child. "She's young, but she's very mature," they would say. "She behaves like a grown-up." There is now a word that describes the reality of young African girls who are robbed of their childhood: "adultification." I was going to be a good woman and a good wife, because I was hardworking and could carry heavy loads.

Girls aged five to nine around the world spend an average of almost four hours a week on household chores—30 percent more time than boys the same age. My brother used to read books and study while I was taking care of chores. In some regions, girls spend much more time on housework: in Somalia, Ethiopia, and Rwanda, more than half of girls aged 5–14 spend at least 14 hours a week, or over two hours a day, helping around the house.[1] Although children aged 5–11 are considered laborers if they spend one hour a week on paid work, household chores are not considered child labor. This means that a five-year-old girl could spend almost four hours a day collecting water and firewood, cleaning, preparing meals, or looking after siblings or sick adults and still not be recognized as a child laborer—and therefore not be granted the same protection as a five-year-old who engages in economic activities for one hour a week.[2]

For many African girls, however, household chores are not the only workload. When I became minister for gender, child welfare, and community services in 2004, the American ambassador called me. "If Malawi keeps trafficking children like this, we will withdraw financial assistance," he said. This is how I found out that Malawi was on the United States tier 2 watch list for human trafficking.

How could this be? I was stunned. Surely he was mistaken. "No. That's not possible. Not in Malawi. We're not selling our children. We're not sending our children abroad," I told him. "There is no trafficking in Malawi."

"Yes, there is," he insisted. "Child labor is trafficking. Child prostitution is trafficking."

Then I woke up. If child labor was considered trafficking, then it was happening a lot in Malawi. A comprehensive child labor survey carried out in 2002 revealed that 37 percent of children aged 5–15 were involved in child labor.[3] Over half of these laboring children worked in agriculture, including tobacco or tea estates. Although Malawi had ratified various international treaties toward the protection and rights of children, there were gaps in our domestic laws, as well as in our ability to enforce them.

Over one in five African children—72 million of them—are considered laborers, meaning they are engaged work that is dangerous or harmful and that interferes with their schooling. This is more than in any other region, in both relative and absolute terms. In spite of efforts to combat it, sub-Saharan Africa has recorded an increase in child labor since 2012, unlike any other major region. Agriculture—mainly subsistence or commercial farming as well as herding—accounts for 85 percent of child labor in Africa.[4] Most of these children are not employed outside their homes: they work on their parents' farm or fishing enterprise—and are unpaid.[5]

Work often starts at an early age: in rural Malawi, over 60 percent of girls in child labor start working before age nine.[6] Children aged 5–11 account for 48 percent of all child laborers in the world, and close to half of them are girls.[7] Together with subsistence or commercial farming, domestic work in homes other than their own—a type of child labor that often goes unreported[8]—is the most common occupation for African girls. This is unfortunately not unusual: two-thirds of child domestic workers in the world are girls[9] who are younger than 12.[10]

So girls are more likely than boys to shoulder a double burden: both working and performing household chores.[11] When taking into account household chores and child labor, the girl child in sub-Saharan Africa shoulders a much heavier workload than does the boy. The workload is heaviest for rural girls: in Guinea, those aged 6–14 have been found to spend an average of 23 hours a week working—over three hours a day—compared to seven hours for girls the same age in urban areas.[12] Most of that time is spent on domestic chores and on family farming.[13]

Why do so many village girls in Africa work so much? Part of it is infrastructure. If there is no electricity, no gas, and no running water, someone has to go draw water and collect firewood. In rural Malawi, only 2 percent of children have piped water in their homes, and 6 percent have electricity, compared to 34 percent and 36 percent in cities.[14] The village woman already works many hours a day growing food, cooking meals, or washing, and she needs help looking after her five, six, or more children. So she teaches her daughter to do such work from a young age, not only because she needs help, but also because her daughter will most likely marry young and must know how to work. This is how girls in rural Africa are conditioned from a very young age. In sub-Saharan Africa, a round trip to collect water takes an average of 33 minutes in rural areas and 25 minutes in towns.[15] Basic infrastructure would save hours of daily work for African women and girls.

So would smaller families. But when I ask a village woman whether she thinks eight children might be enough, her response is always the same. "You have houses and cars," she says. "I have children." First, she thinks she must have eight, because she might lose four. And, mired in dire poverty, she also sees children as wealth. They are extra pairs of hands to work. They are also old-age insurance. They work in the fields and help grow more food, or they do piecework and bring some money home. And if she's lucky, perhaps one of them will end up becoming a teacher or a nurse.

Yet it is also mind-set and tradition. While girls are groomed from a young age to be hardworking and to break their backs carrying heavy pails of water and babies, boys often don't have to do the same amount of work. In many African villages, the boy goes and sits under the tree with the men to eat, listen to the radio, or discuss what is happening in the village. In most African traditions, he is entitled to order grown women around. He is brought up to believe that, because he is male, he is allowed to behave that way. I remember a 14-year-old boy in my husband's village who marched up to a group of married women peeling cassava. "Come and cook for me," he ordered one woman. "It's time for my lunch."

In most of Africa, women do not enjoy the same power as in my matrilineal tradition. They do not own assets, and they are expected to do most of the work. Before I married my second husband, his sister interviewed me. I will never forget the very first question she asked:

"Will you be able to work for him and for us? Will you manage?"

In her patrilineal tradition, I was expected to work and cook for everyone. I was a professional woman by then, and I suggested employing someone.

"No, no, no. It's not the same," I was told.

"What is not the same?" I asked. Surely it did not matter who peeled and cooked the cassava.

"It's not the same when other people are cooking, and not you. It's not the same."

Every chance I get, I stand up to such a mind-set, upset by the injustice that women and girls face. My favorite song is one that people started singing when I became minister: "Don't abuse your wife, Joyce Banda is angry." When I was already in government, I drove to a village one day, and I saw a woman and her husband walking by the side of the road, on their way to visit another village. The woman was balancing a basket of flour on her head, and she was carrying a chicken. And the man? The man, who was wearing a suit, had taken off his shoes—they were hurting his feet as he walked—and had handed them over to his poor wife. He was just walking.

I stopped the car. "What are you doing to your wife?" I asked him. "Pick up your own shoes!"

"Mind your own business!" he said, visibly angry.

"I'll take a photograph of you, and I'll expose you on TV," I said. "I'll tell about you on the radio!"

He was having none of it. "Who are you to tell me how I should treat my wife?"

Another man who cycled past heard our argument. "You don't know her?" he laughed. "She's Joyce Banda!"

The barefoot man, still grumbling, snatched his shoes from his wife's hands and put them back on. The saddest thing was that this poor woman, who was carrying a heavy basket, a chicken, and her husband's shoes while he strolled empty-handed, didn't think there was anything wrong. In her mind, if her husband's shoes were hurting him, then she had to carry them, along with everything else.

This is how the African girl child is conditioned from a young age, and by the time she reaches adolescence, that view of her own worth and of her role in the world is already deeply ingrained. Consequences are both manifold and long-lasting for her and for her community. Of course, helping around the home is part of family life, and there is nothing wrong with that. Yet when this burden becomes excessive and unfairly distributed, it places the girl child at a serious disadvantage. A third of children aged 5–14 considered as laborers do not attend school.[16] Even when they do, their work load gets in the way of studying. Initial research suggests that having to perform household chores for 21 hours a week or more undermines children's ability to attend and benefit from schooling, and girls account for two-thirds of the 54 million children aged 5–14 who do that much housework around the world. While girls under 14 years of age spend on average 34 percent more time working than do boys, the gap widens to 53 percent when comparing children attending school.[17] This confirms that girls are at a greater disadvantage compared to boys even when they are enrolled in school: they are often tired from their chores and caretaker roles at home, which also leave them with far less time to study.

Because household chores fall predominantly on girls, this also means their work burden is not properly recognized and accounted for in existing data and efforts to eradicate child labor. This reinforces a bias that already undervalues girls' and women's contribution around the house, as it is unpaid work. By the time girls turn 10 years old, many are already conditioned to think that this is the role they are meant to fulfill, undermining their self-worth and confidence. They have also been robbed of much-needed time to play and socialize with other children.

As I have experienced myself, working from a young age often leads to injuries. I am the eldest and also the shortest in my family; my youngest sister, who didn't have to carry a baby on her back or firewood and water on her head, and also benefited from better nutrition than myself, is the tallest. I don't believe this is accidental. Young girls often get injured while collecting water and firewood, and also risk sexual violence while walking back and forth.[18] A number of surveys in other regions have confirmed that children working as domestic workers are exposed to significant hazards, ranging from overwork, physical abuse, and sexual exploitation to burns, cuts, exposure to toxic chemicals, and skeletomuscular injuries from carrying heavy loads.[19] Farming, the other main workload for African girls, is more hazardous for children than any other form of child labor.[20] Children involved in tobacco production, for instance, have been found to endure physical abuse, health hazards, long hours for little pay, and sexual abuse, particularly girls.[21]

I am luckier than most: my spine has suffered, but my education and my spirit have not. I have always believed that girls and women make great leaders. I do believe it because I come from a matrilineal tradition, in which women own assets and have power, and my grandmother was a strong woman and role model. And I believe it because my father himself felt that his daughters were destined to do great things and refused to let tradition stand in our way.

3

Sexual Violence and Harmful Traditions

When I was minister for gender, child welfare, and community services, my principal secretary came into my office and announced that there was a nine-year-old girl waiting to see me. I sat the girl down in my office, and she told me her story. She explained that about a year earlier, her mother had traveled to their village in the south, five hours away from Lilongwe, where the family lived, to seek traditional treatment from a witch doctor for her epileptic child. She was gone for a year. While her mother was away, her father walked into her room one night.

"Oh, don't worry," he said. "I'm looking for money."

The girl got up to get dressed and help him look for money.

"No, no," her father then said, "You don't understand. The money is you. I went to a witch doctor today, and the witch doctor told me that my barber shop shall prosper—if I sleep with my girl child."

The young girl started crying for her mother.

"There is no need," her father told her. "I have arranged this with your mother. That's why she is away."

The abuse continued throughout the mother's absence, and still the father's business did not prosper. One day, he tricked her into coming to his barber shop and raped her there, because the witch doctor told him he had to defile her in his place of business. Her father warned her not to tell anybody, or her mother would die. So she suffered in silence. She did not go to the hospital, even though she had suffered serious injuries by then. This eight-year-old was convinced that nobody cared.

Then her mother came back. "Why did you allow this to happen to me?" the girl asked her.

Her mother had no idea. When she confronted her husband, he beat her up. She went to her church to seek help from her pastor.

The pastor advised her to stay quiet. This happened in a lot of families, he told her, and she would not gain anything by exposing her husband. She didn't know where else to go or what else to do. Her husband was so angry that she had reported him to the church that he refused to pay tuition for their daughter. That's when the girl came to my office: she had heard that the Joyce Banda Foundation was sending girls to school, and she wanted to know whether I could help.

I asked her mother whether she could tell her story on TV. "I have nothing to lose," she said. "I've lost my child; she will never be the same. I can't beat my husband up. I can't punish him any other way. The best I can do is tell everybody." The husband was arrested the next day on charges of defilement.

Across sub-Saharan Africa, as everywhere in the world, millions of children are suffering from gender-based violence. Yet girls disproportionately bear the brunt of it. The impact on their physical and mental health is devastating and long-lasting. The nine-year-old who came to my office suffered from significant physical injuries, and some of the damage was irreversible. Besides potentially fatal gynecological complications and internal injuries, young girls are exposed to sexually transmitted diseases, including HIV/AIDS, and, for pubescent girls, unwanted pregnancies. The invisible damage is just as severe. The trauma, helplessness, and, when the violence is perpetrated by a family member, the sense of betrayal leave lifelong scars. Anxiety, low self-esteem, and depression are among the many debilitating consequences.[1]

Violence against young girls is a significant obstacle to their education. According to UNICEF, severe abuse often weighs not only on children's development, but also on their ability to learn and their performance at school.[2] Attending school itself often exposes young girls to harassment, insecurity, and violence. According to a study by Plan International, at least one-third of all child rapes in South Africa in a given time period were committed by school staff.[3]

The full extent of this scourge is difficult to quantify and document. Most of it is hidden, and available evidence is fragmented and anecdotal. Victims are too young or too vulnerable to report it, and often do not know where to turn. The brave nine-year-old girl who walked into my office is a rare exception. Interviewing children, particularly about such sensitive topics, is fraught with legal and practical challenges. In cases of traditional practices, parents and relatives endorse the abuse, which they consider a rite of passage. Definitions of what constitutes sexual violence also vary, making evidence gathering and comparisons challenging.

Yet available evidence suggests that sexual violence against children, which affects girls more than boys, is alarmingly high.[4] National surveys conducted in Kenya, Tanzania, Swaziland, and Zimbabwe suggest that one in three girls experience sexual abuse during their childhood.[5] Incest, trafficking, and the sexual exploitation of child domestic workers is rife. Girls, particularly in rural areas, are married off before they reach adulthood—or even adolescence: 12 percent of sub-Saharan African women aged 20–24 were married or in unions before age 15. In Chad, Niger, and the Central African Republic, child marriage is reported to be as high as 72–78 percent,[6] with 28–29 percent of girls married before they turn 15.[7]

Although most girls having suffered sexual violence report that first instances occurred when they were 15–19 years old, a substantial share experience violence at a younger age.[8] So while the risk worsens as girls age, it is very much present before they turn 10. When I inaugurated a shelter for abused women, I found a young woman whose husband had been defiling their 18-month-old daughter for a year—until a neighbor, worried about the constant crying, broke in and found the husband in the act. He took away the young woman and her baby, who died of AIDS a few months later. Sexual violence against girls is frequently perpetrated in homes, schools, and immediate environments, and is exacerbated in situations of conflict and displacement.[9]

In addition, harmful cultural practices normalize and even encourage violence against young girls, who are most vulnerable to such violence at ages 0–10. Cultural rights are strongly protected in our constitutions, especially given the legacy of colonization, and safeguard our identities as Africans. Yet some of these cultural practices hold the continent back by holding girls down. Attention has focused on female genital mutilation, which, although retreating, is still perpetrated on millions of African girls—mainly in rural areas and among the poorest[10]—typically younger than five.[11] Yet Africa is a vast and diverse continent, and many other harmful practices, which are often very localized within a country or even within a district, have not received as much attention because they are not well known or documented. In Cameroon, for instance, breast ironing is intended to delay sexual activity, and in Ghana, the *trokosi* tradition requires that young girls typically aged 6–10 be enslaved in local shrines to atone for their families' perceived sins.

Malawi is home to a number of harmful traditions. When I was minister of gender, child welfare, and community services in 2006, I visited Nsondole in Malawi's Zomba District for The Hunger Project–Malawi's HIV/AIDS community day. Fourteen young girls and boys had formed a club to speak up against sexual practices in their village. In my interaction with them, I met with two sisters—one nine years old and the other just four. The older sister was telling me about the sores on her skin. The year before, their aunt, who had cared for the girls ever since their parents passed away, had hired a local man—known as a "hyena"—to "cleanse" her under a custom known as *kuchotsa fumbi*. As a feature of initiation ceremonies in parts of southern Malawi, an older man is hired to have sex with a girl at the cusp of puberty, usually between 8 and 12 years old, to cleanse her of childhood and prevent infertility. In this child's situation, she was told the cleansing would guarantee her beautiful skin. Now, with her sores, she did not understand why her skin was no longer smooth like that of her younger sister, who had yet to be cleansed. Not only had this child been raped, but she had also likely been infected with an STD. According to Action Aid and the U.S. Department of State, in parts of northern Malawi, young girls as young as five are forced into sexual relationships with older men in exchange for a loan or livestock, a practice known as *kupimbira*.[12]

African women leaders and international partners have worked hard to bring various forms of harmful traditional practices to light, and many of the gains we have made so far in fighting practices like female genital mutilation and child marriage have been precisely due to their visibility.

Besides harmful traditional practices, attitudes toward women and traditional gender roles contribute to sexual violence. These attitudes become ingrained at a young age, with consequences that will last throughout girls' lives. When girls are socialized from the day they are born to be obedient, subservient, and to please men, much damage has been done by the time they reach adolescence. The way they view themselves, their own worth, and their rights has been shaped. This is why many adolescent girls who have suffered from violence do not report it or seek help to end it, because they do not view it as a problem; in fact, a majority of African adolescent girls—often a higher proportion than boys the same age—believe that a husband or partner is sometimes justified in hitting or beating his wife.[13] Unless they are taught otherwise from a young age and have access to protection or recourse against their abusers, girls grow up accepting that violence is to be expected throughout their lives. Indeed, over 45 percent of African women can expect to be beaten, choked, burned, raped, or abused in some other way during their lifetime, overwhelmingly at the hands of an intimate partner.[14]

I am one of these women. I left my first husband because he was abusive. I had an education and I had a job, and unlike many other women, at least I had the means to leave him and take our three children with me. Unlike many other women, I had also been brought up as a very young girl to believe that I deserved better and that I was strong enough to walk away. Even after we were separated, my husband kept harassing me. One night he came to my house again, drunk, and banged on my door. But that day he did not want to leave. "I'm going to kill you, and I'm going to kill the children!" he kept screaming. I called my father, who was a retired policeman, and he alerted the local police station. I woke up my children and pushed them through the back window so they could escape and hide at a neighbor's house. I went to the kitchen door to leave, but my estranged husband was busy breaking it to get inside. The door fell as I approached it and it hit me. My nose started bleeding, but I manage to run outside. Then I fell and broke my arm. I kept running with a broken arm until I reached the police station.

The policemen, who had been alerted by my father, drove me back to the house in a van with police dogs. By the time we got there, my husband had destroyed everything in my house. Every window, every plate, every cup was broken. By then, my neighbors had gathered around, alerted by the commotion, and my estranged husband was addressing them.

I shall always remember what he then said:

"So tell me, ladies and gentlemen, is it wrong for me to feel jealousy? She's going to get remarried! I know there is a man who wants to marry her!"

The policeman turned to me. "Is this a family matter?"

That was it. Within a few minutes, I went from victim to villain, and my abusive husband went from criminal to hero. I explained that we had been separated for a year, but it didn't matter. We were not officially divorced yet. The police dogs and the uniformed officers got back in the van, and off they went. And that man who had destroyed everything in my house and threatened to kill me and my children? He drove to the police station in his car to give a statement, and I was taken in the police van. Legally, he was still my husband, and the police would not get involved. There was total disregard for my children, then aged four to eight, who were hiding in fear of being killed by their own father. Even my own mother kept telling me to reconcile with him. She could not bear the shame of a daughter divorcing her husband, regardless of how abusive he was. The next day, I went to court to get a divorce.

That episode taught me firsthand that laws, and how they are implemented, matter a great deal. Without proper rules, there can be no proper protection. All African countries except Somalia have endorsed the UN Convention on the Rights of the Child, which legally binds them to protect children's rights, including all forms of sexual exploitation and abuse.[15] Yet many countries have not yet fully translated that commitment into domestic laws, and those that have often struggle to implement these laws, hamstrung by limited resources and poor infrastructure, as well as entrenched cultural practices and attitudes.

In many African countries, the law also fails to recognize the concept of marital rape, which goes against the widespread attitude that men are entitled to sex. This is how young girls are brought up, and by the time they reach adolescence and adulthood, they often believe this too. When pushing the Domestic Violence Bill through Parliament, we tried to include it. I went to the leader of the largest opposition party in Parliament and made the case for the bill, asking for his party's support. "This bill is good for women, this bill is good for children, and this bill is good for yourself," I told him. "This protects everyone in the household." This is why the bill covered "domestic" rather than "gender-based" violence. "I will support you if you take out this clause," he told me. "Because this is not in our culture. How can a woman say no to her husband?" In the end, I had to drop marital rape. I cried so much over this. I cried out of frustration and anger. I cried out of sadness for my sisters throughout the country. I cried for their daughters, who were growing up believing this was part of life and part of being married. I felt I was betraying them and betraying my country. But ultimately, I had a choice to make. Would I stand firm and see the bill fail altogether? Or would I retreat for now and push for what I could? I decided to look at the Domestic Violence Bill as a first step. It was incomplete, but it was better than nothing at all.

Drafting laws is only a first step. All too often, entrenched cultural practices, as my own experience has taught me, undermine their relevance. More recently, this was painfully apparent in the case of Eric Aniva, a "hyena" from southern Malawi. Besides being hired to have sex with newly bereaved widows and women struggling to get pregnant, "hyenas" are also "cleansing" young girls, some as young as five years old—failing which some kind of misfortune could supposedly hit their family and village. Aniva boasted to the BBC that he had slept with over 100 women and young girls, whose relatives hired him.[16] He also shared with journalists that he was HIV-positive, a fact he had not disclosed to his "clients." The international exposure created national embarrassment, and he was arrested. Yet he was sentenced to only two years in prison with hard labor on charges of "harmful cultural practice," after two newly bereaved widows he had "cleansed" came forward.[17] How can a "hyena" get only a two-year sentence for what he did? Because no girl or parent came forward to testify against him.

These beliefs and attitudes take root before girls turn 10, and interventions are required to protect very young girls against violence and harmful traditions—and the beliefs and mind-set that make it easier for them to endure those traditions. For violence and harmful traditions, besides the harm they inflict directly on the girl child, also create additional obstacles to the single most powerful tool that can propel young girls on the path to leadership: education.

4

Valuing Education

Education meant everything to my father, because he was denied education himself. When his mother became widowed and remarried, her well-to-do second husband wanted nothing to do with her two sons. Although my father's mother had another three children and lived in town with her new family, her older sons—my father and his brother—had to stay in the village. Every morning, my father walked seven kilometers to go to school in town, walking past his mother's house. And every evening he walked back. My father dropped out of school after the fourth grade: no one would pay his school fees. Eventually, he joined the police force's band and taught himself music. I still remember him studying through the night while he was working. Music grade one, music grade two, music grade three. He passed all his exams. By sheer force of will and hard work, he got a scholarship to go study in the UK. When he came back, he was the only African teaching at the prestigious Kamuzu Academy in Malawi. This is how far he went on his own, starting from nothing.

He made sure his own children understood the value of education. "I did not get an opportunity to go to school," he used to tell us every single day. "But I will make sure you go. The education I was denied, you will have." Every day, he pushed us. He made us listen to classical music and read about Beethoven and Handel—which bored us to tears. He made us read one book a day. Boy or girl, it did not matter to him: all his children would be educated and be given the same opportunity. He was an exception, and his friends would mock him for sending his girls to school. "Are you trying to turn them into boys?" they would say. He didn't care. "Don't lose this opportunity," he kept telling us. "There are so many without it."

Much progress has been achieved since I was a young girl. More African girls are getting an education than ever before. Over three-quarters of girls of primary school age in the region now go to school, compared to just half in 1995.[1] In countries such as Ghana, net primary school enrollment is above 90 percent.

The benefits of educating girls are well known: girls who stay in school longer typically have better earning prospects, marry later, and have fewer children. Their own children are healthier and better educated. So girls' schooling now features high on governments' and donors' agendas. A recent survey of policymakers in five developing countries, including Kenya and Senegal, confirmed that education stands out as the most often cited priority in policies seeking to reduce the gender gap. In fact, over 8 in 10 policymakers thought that gender equality was given a high or very high priority in education policy.[2]

So with all that progress and attention, why should we include education in interventions targeting girls aged 0–10?

First, because we have not yet reached universal primary education, and a gender gap, although narrower, persists, particularly in sub-Saharan Africa. In spite of rapid progress, net girl enrollment in primary schools in sub-Saharan Africa still trails behind all other regions. Across sub-Saharan Africa, there are still over 18 million girls of primary school age who are out of school—3 million more than boys the same age and a staggering 58 percent of the world's total.[3] About half of these out-of-school girls—9 million, compared to 6 million boys—will never go at all, while a third will, but late; another 17 percent have been schooled but dropped out.[4] The inequity between boys' and girls' enrollment is wider in sub-Saharan Africa than anywhere else.

Second, aggregate numbers hide significant disparities, all of which leave poor rural girls at a disadvantage. Over three-quarters of primary-age girls in South Sudan are out of school, compared to less than 5 percent in Zimbabwe, Kenya, or Gabon.[5] Disparities within countries are also significant. For instance, 55 percent of children are out of primary school in rural Niger, compared to 17 percent in cities. Similar disparities are recorded in

Guinea, Burkina Faso, and Mali, while the divide between rural and urban in Kenya, Zimbabwe, and Gabon is almost nonexistent.[6] Distance from school and poor education quality all weigh on rural girls, who are the most likely to miss out on school.

The cost of education, even when primary education is free, still weighs heavily on access. I remember when, in 1994, Malawi's President Muluzi fulfilled one of his campaign promises to make primary education free in Malawi. It felt like a dream—even though the president did not give much thought to infrastructure, desks, books, or teachers. Yet even with primary education now free in most of sub-Saharan Africa, schooling often remains beyond the reach of the poorest, who cannot afford school uniforms, transport, or books.

Income level is indeed related to the widest disparities in enrollment, particularly for girls. In other words, wealthier families are far more likely than the poorest ones not only to send—and keep—their children in school, but also to treat girls and boys more equally. Almost half of the poorest African children are out of primary school, compared to 1 in 10 of the wealthiest. Nowhere is the wealth gap wider than in Nigeria, where 71 percent of the poorest children are out of primary school, compared to 1 percent for the wealthiest. A wealthy urban child in Nigeria—boy or girl—averages around 10 years of schooling, while poor rural Hausa girls average less than six months.[7]

Population growth compounds the impact of poverty on young girls' education. In Malawi, the average woman has more than four children,[8] and children are still considered free labor or a source of income. When faced with the direct and indirect cost of sending these children to school, a choice has to be made. Can I afford to send any of my children to school? And if I cannot afford to send all of them, then who am I going to send first? Boys are typically favored, because girls are expected to get married and have children. So why do they need an education? This reality prevails even in my own matriarchal tradition.

In addition, enrollment data fails to tell the whole story. Even for the girl child who is signed up for school, the battle is only half won. Being able to stay in school, show up every day, and make the most of it is another challenge altogether. As discussed in earlier chapters, a girl child who is poor and lives in rural areas often does not eat as much or as well as her brother, which affects her ability to focus and learn. She is more likely to face violence, a trauma that also affects her education. And if she must clean the house, grow food, cook for everybody in the house, look after the sick or the younger children, or do piecework to bring some money home, she is more likely to miss some school days. Even if she manages to attend, she is so tired that she is unable to make the most of her time at school. She also has less time to do homework.

I once invited the Japanese ambassador to visit the Joyce Banda Foundation in Domasi, Zomba. He visited a family headed by a young girl. Both parents had died of AIDS, and this young girl had to look after her younger siblings and do everything in the house. She had to do piecework to feed her family. She had little to eat. Then she walked several kilometers to go to school. By the time she was in class, she was so exhausted that she was dozing off—and the ambassador decided to fund the building of a hostel for girls. Statistically, that girl is in school. But how much of an education is she receiving? And how long before she drops out because the burden of responsibilities weighing on her shoulders is so heavy? In West Africa, for instance, multiple roles have been shown to be responsible for girls failing to complete their formal education.[9] And households with many younger siblings have a negative effect on girls' schooling.[10] Although girls around the world tend to do better than boys in school, the few countries where girls were found to repeat grades more than boys are mostly in sub-Saharan Africa.[11]

In addition, interventions should target girls aged 0–10 because their attitude toward education is shaped at a very young age, well before they reach adolescence. That attitude will help keep them in school—or will instead nudge them to walk away. And the rural girl who does not go to secondary school is not going to stay in her family home: she will be married well before she turns 18—even when there is a law against it.

She will need a mind-set that deeply values education to stay in school, because challenges to education pile up as poor and rural girls grow older. There are good reasons for gender interventions to target adolescents: the rate of out-of-school girls increases at the secondary level, with 36 percent of adolescents not enrolled in lower secondary education and 61 percent out of upper secondary.[12] And a significant proportion of adolescent girls who do go to school attend primary education, often because they started late.[13] Some of the root causes are the same as in primary school: the gender gap in enrollment between the wealthiest and the poorest widens in secondary education. Although most African countries offer free primary education, secondary school often requires tuition. This is what cost my friend Chrissie her future. Although she was a brilliant student and had been selected to attend the best secondary school in the country, she dropped out after one term because her family could not afford the six-dollar tuition.

Distance and the poor quality of education are often more acute problems at the secondary level. So is poor sanitation. A young girl who starts menstruating is often ashamed to go to school. She often does not know what is happening. She is scared, and nobody has told her what she is supposed to do about it. She doesn't have sanitary pads—or doesn't know that such a thing exists. This is one of the many issues that her mother is not supposed to discuss with her, according to tradition. So the girl is afraid she will mess up her clothes and be ridiculed, and unless she has access to a proper toilet or to sanitary pads, she does not want to go to school. How often does this happen? In Malawi, for instance, 20–25 percent of government schools have an average of only one latrine for 150 pupils.[14] One in 10 school-age African girls are thought to not attend school during menstruation—about 20 percent of the school year.[15]

Yet even interventions successfully targeting these external obstacles—from cash transfers and school feeding programs to scholarships and proper sanitation—while effective, cannot keep all girls in school. This suggests that educating girls is still too often perceived as having little value—including by girls themselves. How much do such attitudes weigh on enrollment, compared to other factors? We need to gather more evidence on attitudes toward education of girls themselves, as well as parents, teachers, and communities at large. But it is a significant obstacle, and it starts early. This is why interventions should start well before girls turn 10, when the seeds of such inequalities are planted, bearing consequences that become fully apparent later in life.

Mind-set starts with families and communities. How can girls be expected to value their own education if their families or communities do not? My father's attitude toward education shaped mine from the moment I was born. Parents and other family members play the deciding role in whether or not children go to school, even when it is available.[16] Inspiring and supporting girls to go to school—much as my father did with us—is essential. In fact, women leaders interviewed by *The Atlantic* partly attributed their drive to lead to father figures who encouraged them to study and speak up.[17] Much work has to be done with teachers as well: although many teachers claim to treat boys and girls equally, studies of rural pupils in Kenya, Malawi, and Rwanda have revealed that their attitudes are often biased, and their expectations low for girl students.[18] A study in Uganda found that teachers reinforced the orientation of girls toward women-dominated industries.[19]

If families, teachers, and communities are crucial in shaping young girls' ambitions and their attitude toward education, so are role models. My father would say to anyone who had gone to secondary school, "Can you please come home and meet my children? They must see somebody who has gone to secondary." If girls are able to see from a young age where education can take them, they are less likely to drop out. Why would young girls want to stay in school if all the older girls they know don't go, and get married at 15? Early marriage and pregnancy may account for 20 percent of dropouts—with early marriage having a larger effect than childbirth.[20]

Gender stereotypes blunt girls' schooling ambitions. If women around them, particularly their mothers and aunties, are trapped in traditional roles of household work and caregiving, this is likely to be the only future they can imagine for themselves right from the start, particularly if their own families and communities reinforce these stereotypical roles. If these roles have been drummed into their young minds when these minds are the most malleable, it will be difficult for them to envisage anything else by the time they turn 10. In West Africa, the typical representation of women in textbooks as housewives, traders, and low-income workers—while men are represented as heroes, leaders, or holding prestigious jobs—has been found to contribute to girls dropping out of school at high rates.[21] Girls and women in mathematics textbooks in Cameroon, Côte d'Ivoire, and Togo accounted for less than 30 percent of all characters.[22] The number of women teachers is correlated to girls' enrollment and achievement, particularly in sub-Saharan Africa, in part because they are role models.[23] To me, the most valuable legacy of my presidency is that young girls in Malawi are now able to imagine that they too could become a minister or head of state one day.

Girls also directly benefit from having mothers who are better educated and better able to influence decisions within their household. When women contribute toward the family income and also have influence on how that income gets spent, their daughters are more likely to go to and stay in school. Too often I have talked to village women who have told me, "I don't want my child to be ignorant like me, but I don't know what to do because

I don't earn any money." Their husbands decide who will go to school. Children—particularly girls—living in households headed by women are more likely to be in school and to have completed grade four when compared with other families of the same socioeconomic conditions.[24] There is clear evidence linking women's education level and school enrollment for their children, particularly girls. So interventions supporting mothers' financial independence heavily influence the girl child's ability to go to and stay in school, which in turn will help her own daughters, should she have any, later in life.

Legal instruments would also help. Mandatory education has been shown to improve enrollment and education achievement, particularly for girls.[25] Yet the guideline of 12 years of compulsory education remains the exception rather than the rule in sub-Saharan Africa, where in some countries, including Malawi, education is not mandatory, even at the primary level (see Figure 1). Legal requirements would nudge parents who do not see any value in educating their girls to send them to school anyway—provided, of course, that schooling is made accessible. If education is not free, or there aren't enough schools, then it cannot be made compulsory.

Figure 1. Duration of Compulsory Education (excluding pre-primary education), 2014

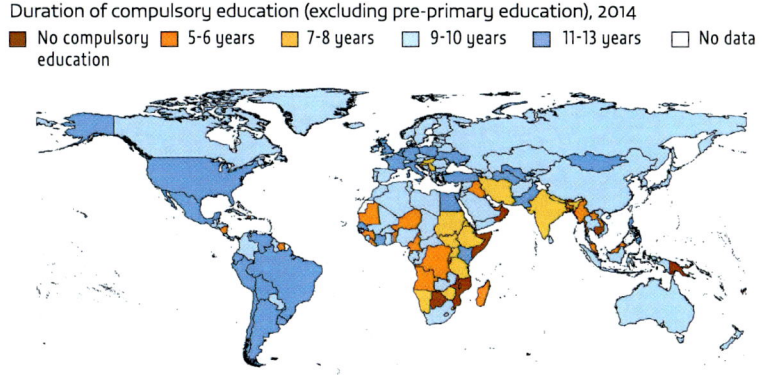

Source: UNESCO Institute for Statistics (UIS), Leaving No One Behind: How Far on the Way to Universal Primary and Secondary Education?, https://en.unesco.org/gem-report /leaving-no-one-behind-how-far-way-universal-primary-and-secondary-education#, 2016.

So mind-set and attitudes are sometimes the greatest obstacles of all. And this mind-set is shaped before girls turn 10, even though its consequences might become fully apparent only later in life, when an adolescent girl drops out of school. It is during their early years that girls are taught to become subservient and to stunt their ambitions. It is before they turn 10 that they can be taught to believe that their sole purpose is to get married and bear children, and that education has little value in that future. My husband's older sister used to carry her brothers' suitcases to the bus station when they went to school. Her father was the very first to own a car in his community, and the family could afford the tuition for her and her sisters as well. Yet she decided not to go, unlike her other siblings. Why? Because in spite of her family's means, she came to believe from an early age that her role in life would not require much education: she would get married and have children, so why did she need to study? She did indeed get married, but she also got divorced. And while one brother became a chief justice and the other a diplomat, she worked as a cleaner in a hospital because she had not studied past primary school.

My fate could easily have been my village friend Chrissie's were it not for my father, and the education he gave me.

Joyce Banda surrounded by children from the Joyce Banda Foundation Primary School in Blantyre, Malawi.

Credit: Joyce Banda Foundation

A small girl carries firewood in the Democratic Republic of Congo. In much of Africa, young girls spend several hours a week collecting wood.

Credit: Ollivier Girard/CIFOR/Flickr

A young girl carries her infant sister. In Somalia, Ethiopia, and Rwanda, more than half of girls aged 5–14 spend at least 14 hours a week on household chores like collecting water and firewood, cleaning, cooking, and looking after siblings.
Credit: Sarah Diederich/Flickr

Near the village of Melbana in Ethiopia, a girl hauls water in a jerrycan strapped to her back. In sub-Saharan Africa, a round trip to collect water takes an average of 33 minutes in rural areas.

Credit: UNICEF Ethiopia/2011/Lemma/Flickr

Child marriage is unlawful in many African countries, including Malawi, but it is still widespread.
Credit: Thomas Cockrem/Alamy Stock Photo

A group of girls watch their mother prepare food in Mali. In much of rural Africa, boys and men eat first and best.
Credit: Jake Lyell/Almay Stock Photo

Part II
Interventions

5

Invest in Data and Evidence

If we are to progress further toward gender equality, adding to the valuable initiatives focusing on women and adolescent girls by developing a policy agenda supporting girls aged 0–10 is critical. The previous chapters have made the case that gender inequality does not start at adolescence. African girls, particularly in rural areas, are disadvantaged from day one in several critical areas, from nutrition and unpaid household work to sexual violence, harmful traditions, and education. Even in areas where inequality becomes more pronounced during adolescence or adulthood, the seeds of inequality are firmly planted in the minds of young girls, which become fertile grounds for future discrimination. In order to level the playing field, we cannot afford to wait until girls reach their teenage years.

The first step is to build solid evidence to properly measure that disadvantage, clearly identify causes, and then design and evaluate interventions supporting the girl child from birth. Proper qualitative and quantitative evidence is essential to influence policy and mobilize resources. To properly ascertain scale, scope, and priorities, we need data. Then, once interventions are in place, data and evidence are also essential to measure what works and what doesn't, prioritize resources, and track progress.

Yet there is a dearth of data on women and girls in general, and on young girls in particular. The Sustainable Development Goals include

53 indicators explicitly related to women and girls. Only 15 of these 53 are well defined and available.[1] Evidence documenting the disadvantages that rural African girls experience before they turn 10 is even patchier: data disaggregation by age tends to group boys and girls together, and data related to women and girls often fails to either include girls aged 0–10 or to disaggregate by age. Urban versus rural granularity adds another critical dimension that is often lacking. As a result, the rural girl child becomes largely invisible, appearing only sporadically in statistics, while large swathes of her life remain in the dark.

The previous chapters have highlighted some of these gaps. Girls' enrollment and work considered as child labor, for example, are far better measured and documented than learning achievements, school attendance, and work such as household chores. We also know that gender bias and attitudes influence girls' schooling, but by how much? And besides practices such as female genital mutilation and child marriage, we know too little about sexual violence and harmful traditions, which often remain shrouded in secrecy and social taboo. Whatever data is available is incomplete, unreliable, or sporadic.

In addition, we need better tools to track resources spent on gender interventions. The Organisation for Economic Co-Operation and Development, for instance, has introduced a Gender Equality Policy Marker that tracks bilateral aid spent on closing the gender gap. Yet the data are broken down by donor, by sector of intervention, and by recipient country, but not by age.[2] Rigorous and systematic evaluations are also necessary to measure what works and what doesn't, so interventions can be improved based on solid evidence, and spending channeled more effectively.

In short, we need more, better, and regular data. How do we collect this evidence? By leveraging existing resources, harnessing innovation, and fostering partnerships. A lot can be achieved using existing information and data collection systems. Some of the data and evidence related to girls aged 0–10 is buried in existing databases, but needs to be mined, disaggregated, and analyzed. Of the data that could be mined from existing databases, however, few indicators apply to girls aged 0–10,[3] which highlights the need for collection. Existing data collection tools, such as household surveys, can be improved and broadened to include information about young girls and eliminate gender bias. Survey questions are often tainted by traditional views of gender roles, work, and assumptions that households are headed by men. Such surveys, for instance, capture 75 percent of men's economic activities, but only 30 percent of women's.[4] Improving existing surveys could yield valuable information on young girls in a sustainable and cost-effective manner. This is a first step.

Besides leveraging existing data collection, new and innovative tools can also be developed to collect and analyze data that capture the situation of young girls, their voices and attitudes, as well as the social norms that affect them. One such innovation is the Girl Roster, developed by the Population Council and its partners. The tool kit targets adolescent girls, particularly those in marginalized and poor communities, to reach those who are being left behind. Carefully trained local program staff go door-to-door, asking questions about girls who live in the house, their schooling, whether they are married, and whether they have children. The information is recorded on smartphones and used to create a profile of these girls' lives and needs, and to break them down into meaningful segments.[5] The most off-track girls are then invited to join support groups to connect them with local services and resources to assist them.[6] Similar approaches could be used for programs targeting younger girls.

Young Lives, for instance, is the first longitudinal study of childhood poverty conducted in more than one developing country and covering multiple topics.[7] The study, which has been following the same 12,000 children in Ethiopia, Peru, India, and Vietnam from early infancy into early adulthood, relies on child, household, and community surveys, school surveys, and qualitative research conducted every three years.

Another example of innovation is TechMousso, supported by international partners, a gender data competition in Côte d'Ivoire in which local tech teams propose innovative solutions to gender data challenges identified by local NGOs.[8] One of the winning projects proposed a platform to collect anonymous information on gender-based violence to create a map of incidents that would inform public awareness campaigns.[9] These kinds of initiatives could be harnessed to address some of the challenges related to collecting data on young girls.

Asking adults about young girls, however, misses out on girls' own perceptions. Advancing data and evidence one step further would involve hearing from young girls themselves. In South Africa, for instance, the Girls Achieve Power (GAP) Year Program uses soccer, not only to mentor young girls and boys, but also to gather data directly from them.[10] Similar initiatives could be extended to girls younger than 10, and offer safe spaces in which these young girls can be encouraged to share their stories. Save the Children has launched an initiative to collect children's voices in several countries, which has revealed that children feel that their voices are not being heard.[11] And Young Lives, the longitudinal study of children conducted in four developing countries, relies in part on child questionnaires and school surveys.[12]

At the same time, doing research involving children directly raises practical and ethical challenges. First, such research or evidence collection requires consent from both children and caregivers. How do we ensure that children provide informed consent at such a young age? In addition, parents, community leaders, and even local governments are often reluctant to facilitate such research, particularly on sensitive topics. Save the Children's Young Voices initiative has bumped up against reluctance from schools to allow access to their students. Some administrators wanted to review questions beforehand, and others flatly refused to have any questions related to school. Only when they were assured that schools would not be named did some of them agree.[13]

Second, traditional ways of collecting data from surveys and interviews are not appropriate or effective in gathering information from very young children themselves. Innovative tools based on play and observation need to be further developed. Save the Children's Young Voices survey, for instance, only targets older children aged 12, 14, and 16.[14] Even when children are old enough to be interviewed, a number of factors significantly affect their responses; where the interview takes place, who conducts it, and whether a parent or caregiver is present are likely to influence their answers.

When I was minister, I appointed two child protection officers per constituency, supplied them with bicycles and training, and introduced Children's Corners in some constituencies. On Saturdays, each child protection officer would call all the children in the constituency to a central place where they could play—and get support. In such settings, data could be collected in ways that are not threatening or intimidating for young children.

A third consideration is to ensure the privacy, safety, and confidentiality of children. Their participation in research and evidence collection should not put them in harm's way because of the information they reveal, nor cause emotional distress.

The Ethical Research Involving Children initiative—or ERIC—was created to address such concerns. A partnership among various organizations,[15] ERIC provides guidelines and practical advice on doing research involving children.[16]

Beside innovation, gathering such data and evidence also relies on partnerships. Efforts of this nature and scale require resources and access. The international community can support this effort by providing financial and technical assistance, setting standards, collating data, and sharing best practices, methodology, and findings. Local communities, NGOs, and traditional leaders have a critical role to play in identifying gaps and facilitating data collection, access, and research. In remote rural areas, where the authority of the state often gets significantly diluted, traditional chiefs are the guardians of culture and traditions, and they wield significant power. So do religious leaders. Who will encourage families and local communities to open up? How will young girls who have endured harmful traditional practices be identified? How will the more obscure practices even be documented? How will questionnaires be drafted or alternative methods of data collection that are culturally appropriate and relevant be developed? This requires a level of local understanding and access that only trusted members of these communities can provide.

African governments also have a crucial role to play. There is a significant amount of resistance to collecting data and evidence that would expose and measure sensitive challenges, such as sexual violence and harmful traditional practices. Resistance to such efforts is rooted in shame. Nobody wants to look bad. Yet measurements, transparency, and comparisons are the first step in spurring change. In a different field, the Doing Business survey from the World Bank, for instance, generates momentum in countries keen to improve their ranking and do better than their peers. Regional bodies such as the African Union can be a useful starting point to bring African governments on board by advocating the purpose and benefits of such an investment in data and evidence gathering. It takes a few countries saying yes and leading by example to create peer pressure and nudge others to follow by heaping praise on the trailblazers. The women's focus group at the Pan-African Parliament is well placed to drive that effort within the African Union. Similarly, engaging traditional and community structures at the subnational level is essential. It is a huge task, but I am confident that it can be tackled.

Malawi's Human Rights Commission, for instance, conducted a study of cultural practices by region and was able to catalogue these practices and their incidence through focus group discussions and interviews with randomly selected adults and youth, including traditional and religious leaders.[17] The study, while acknowledging that some respondents were not forthcoming about some cultural practices, nonetheless managed to provide qualitative and quantitative evidence that informed the Malawi Law Commission's regional consultations with traditional leaders during the drafting of the Gender Equality Bill, which included provisions related to these practices. Authorities were then able to design a range of responses, from statutory regulations to negotiations with traditional leaders to modify practices that were found to be harmful.

Momentum has been building at the international level to address the dearth of gender data, and several initiatives and partnerships have emerged. In 2012, the UN Foundation launched Data2X to improve gender data through partnerships. Data2X has now mapped data gaps, but this mapping does not specifically target the 0–10 age group,[18] and, as far as girls are concerned, focuses on adolescents.[19] In 2016, UN Women launched Making Every Woman and Girl Count, a public–private initiative to provide technical and financial support to countries so they can better produce and use gender data.[20] The Bill and Melinda Gates Foundation is committed to spending half of its $80 million gender commitment toward addressing the data gap and is supporting various initiatives.[21] Part of that commitment was to join forces with other international partners to create Equal Measures 2030, a partnership launched in 2017 to close the data gap in order to improve policymaking around gender issues. Efforts to collect rigorous evidence on the impact of gender interventions have also emerged, including What Works,[22] which focuses on violence; the Growth and Opportunity for Women (GrOW) initiative spearheaded by Canada's International Research Center;[23] and the World Bank's Africa Gender Innovation Lab.[24] Yet girls aged 0–10 have received little, if any, attention within these initiatives.

These initiatives offer unprecedented opportunities to build a solid foundation supporting interventions focusing on girls from 0 to 10, and that age group should not be forgotten in these efforts.

Collecting data and evidence is only half the challenge, however. Next is to make sure they get into the hands of those in a position to influence policy, from government officials to NGOs, the media, and the public at large. When Equal Measures 2030 recently surveyed policymakers in five countries, it found that most were ill-informed on gender data—even when data were available. When asked to estimate key measures such as the prevalence of girls getting married before turning 18, for instance, most admitted they did not know, or offered answers that were far off the mark: only a quarter of policymakers came within 20 percent of the most recently available figure.[25] When asked about the proportion of women in Parliament—which is 21 percent—Kenyan politicians' estimates ranged from 6 to 90 percent.[26]

Besides advocating for better and more consistent collection, analysis, and use of gender data, both quantitative and qualitative, covering various ages and stages of girls' and women's lives, Equal Measures 2030 intends to work with rights advocates, NGOs, and decision makers to influence policies and decisions affecting women and girls based on improved evidence.[27] This means better disseminating and communicating the data that already exist and exploring collaborations to fill data gaps.

Only then will we be able to build a more complete and accurate picture of the African girl child, the challenges she faces, and how we can level the playing field—from day one.

6

The Weight of the Law

Collecting data and evidence informs policymaking. Aligning domestic laws to reflect national objectives and international commitments is another necessary intervention to support girls aged 0–10. Promoting gender equality from a very young age requires proper legal tools and recourse.

For the most rural and vulnerable girls, laws can become a strong coalescing point for a wide range of actors to spur positive change. A study estimated that the legislation banning female genital mutilation in Burkina Faso, adopted in 1996, resulted in more than 237,000 women and girls being spared from the practice over a 10-year period.[1] In Ghana, the 1998 law against *trokosi*—or "wife of the gods," a practice by which young girls, usually 6–10 years old, are given indefinitely as slaves to a shrine for an offense committed by a family member—gave local advocacy groups and NGOs a tangible instrument to hold the government accountable and garner support from international partners.[2]

Many African countries now have legal frameworks targeting child labor, gender violence, harmful traditions, and education. Yet there is still much work to do.

First, some gaps, outdated legislation, and loopholes remain, and laws are sometimes too vague or inconsistent. In Malawi, for instance, the law sets the minimum working age at 14—younger than international standards—but it does not cover domestic work, leaving many children, particularly young girls, without formal protection.[3] Also, international or constitutional obligations are often slow to be translated into domestic legislation. Ghana, for instance, only abolished the centuries-old practice of *trokosi* in 1998, though its 1992 constitution and other international laws mandated the eradication of all practices of slavery.[4] In addition, statutory laws and constitutional protections sometimes coexist with customary laws, and are not always consistent:[5] in a number of countries, including Botswana, Ghana, Gambia, Sierra Leone, Lesotho, Mauritius, and Zambia,[6] customary law need not conform to the constitution or any protection or rights it may contain for girls and women.

Second, laws, while helpful, are not sufficient in themselves. Making sure rules translate into reality on the ground requires multipronged interventions. In many African countries, including my own, child marriage, for example, is unlawful, yet the practice is still widespread. According to a recent survey, a quarter of women reported being married before the legal limit in 32 of 50 countries—a proportion much higher in some African countries.[7] A girl who is not in school is particularly vulnerable: what is she going to do? In poor families, she is often looked upon as an extra mouth to feed or, when dowries are practiced, a source of income. There is no way she is going to stay home until she is 18, just because the law says she is not allowed to get married. She's still going to be married off.

Similarly, the case of Eric Aniva, the HIV-positive "hyena" who went on trial in Malawi after boasting to have been paid to have sex with over 100 women and girls, highlighted the limits of the law. Although Malawi has outlawed the harmful traditional practices in which he was engaging, none of the young girls he had "cleansed" or their relatives came forward to testify against him. In the first few years following the legal ban of *trokosi* in Ghana, the government did not make any arrests or prosecute any offenders. Nor did it have a plan to rescue the estimated 4,000 *trokosi* slaves and their estimated 16,000 children from 76 shrines.[8]

Deeply ingrained in identity and a sense of community belonging, these practices are seen as either beneficial by those who practice them or unavoidable due to peer pressure. This explains why female genital mutilation is practiced even in diaspora communities in the UK or the United States. Few women report violence against themselves or their daughters, often because they are financially dependent on their husbands, are afraid of them, or do not know their legal rights.⁹ In some cases, they are also discouraged from doing so by authority figures such as the police or religious and traditional leaders, and do not know where else to go for help. So how can young girls be expected to do so?

If change is to take root, particularly in rural areas, adopting new laws to support and protect the girl child while respecting local traditions cannot happen in a vacuum. Legal reform offers opportunities to talk and debate, mobilize and foster partnerships. To be effective, it must go hand in hand with dialogue and innovation. The banning of female genital mutilation in Burkina Faso, for instance, followed years of advocacy by the government and civil society.¹⁰ Well before the law was adopted, radio announcements, public awareness campaigns, and the establishment of a hotline to support women and girls who were at risk or suffered from complications had laid the groundwork.

Similarly, pushing the Domestic Violence bill through Parliament in Malawi required working with civil society, mobilizing people, and securing support and buy-in from the top. Ahead of the vote in Parliament, we organized a media campaign to expose the problem and how serious it was. To this day, I clearly remember one man who had chopped off his pregnant wife's arms after she'd decided to leave him. "How am I going to hold my baby," the woman kept asking me when I met her. Another woman had had her eye gouged out because she had not cooked the beans her husband had demanded for dinner. A third had run away after her husband aborted several unborn babies he did not want—he had done the same with his previous two wives, who had also escaped. These women told their stories on national television and radio. I was so determined to shed light on this scourge and to mobilize as many people as I could that songs started circulating throughout Malawi: "Don't abuse your wife, Joyce Banda is angry."

Working with civil society, I then organized a march. Ahead of time, I approached the president and cabinet. We were just three women ministers back then. "Mr. President," I said, "I have organized a national march against gender-based violence. It would be very good if my fellow cabinet ministers marched with us." The president asked male ministers to join the march. We even invited the Malawi Police Band. Thousands of people were on the streets that day. At the end of the march, I inaugurated a shelter for abused women. So when it was time to vote on the bill in Parliament, MPs knew that there was popular support behind it, as well as support from the president and cabinet ministers. For several weeks, with the support of Oxfam and the UN Population Fund, I had also been meeting with male MPs to discuss the bill and why Malawi needed it. All this work contributed to a national dialogue and debate. It highlighted a problem and why it was important to solve it. It contributed to shifting attitudes. The same can be done for an agenda focusing on young girls.

Once laws are adopted, people must know about them. How else would they know about girls' rights and be able to take action? It takes translations into local languages, visual and radio information being widely available in rural communities, and awareness campaigns for girls and women to know about the recourses that are available to them. Offering rights education in schools informs young girls about what they are entitled to and where they can find support if they need it.

Besides information, help and support must also be accessible. It is one thing to know your rights, but where are you going to go when you need help? In rural areas, most people have never seen a court of law. Courts are often too far, and far too intimidating. Agents who are supposed to enforce child labor laws are typically short of staff and resources. My own experience with my abusive first husband taught me that the police are often not sympathetic to women and girls. Not much has changed: the U.S. Department of State reports that, although Malawi's police regularly investigated cases of rape and sexual assault, they typically did not intervene in domestic disputes. Also, the police's capacity to document cases of gender violence was limited.[11] A survey of young adults aged 18–24, many of whom had faced violence as children, revealed that less than a quarter knew of a place to seek help against violence.[12]

Some of these challenges can be eased through innovation and training. The Population Council's Girl Roster initiative, for instance, connects vulnerable adolescent girls with the support they need.[13] Could the same be done for younger girls? In Malawi, the Children's Corners established in some constituencies allowed boys and girls not only to come and play safely, but also to talk or seek help if needed.

Incentives and alternatives are also essential to ensure proper implementation of the law while respecting local traditions and culture. Interventions that facilitate girls' education are key to combating child marriage. In Bangladesh, conditional financial incentives have also been effective in reducing child marriage.[14] Traditional practices can also be modified so they are no longer harmful to girls, rather than abandoned or banned altogether. Some traditional initiations, for instance, have been altered to substitute symbolic components for harmful practices on girls. In Kenya, the Naning'oi Boarding School project tapped into a Maasai tradition according to which baby girls are "booked" or promised as wives, sometimes before they are even born. The project substituted for the economic incentives of marrying girls early by "booking" girls for school instead. It enrolled respected community elders to offer gifts as a dowry substitute to a girl's father on behalf of the school—the "suitor"—in exchange for committing to the girl's attendance at the boarding school.[15] In Ghana, shrines were offered cash and material incentives in exchange for *trokosi* slaves.[16]

Fostering dialogue and awareness, making a case for legislation, and ensuring its effective implementation all require partnerships. It starts with enlisting the support of civil society and traditional leaders, particularly in rural areas. To be effective, laws require buy-in, and practices need to be monitored. Rather than defaulting to outright condemnation and criminalization, using the existing power structures at the community level is a powerful way to improve the endorsement and application of laws on the ground. In Ghana, civil society was instrumental in rolling back *trokosi*: International Needs Ghana (ING) worked for decades to raise public awareness and lobby the government to criminalize the practice, and once the legal ban was in place, led rescue efforts.[17]

The international community also has a role to play in setting international legal standards, sharing best practices, assisting legal reform, and providing financial assistance. Commitments and campaigns at the global level support change on the ground. International charters and treaties meant to protect children in general, and girls in particular, against practices that hurt them are setting standards and holding governments accountable for translating their international commitments into domestic legislation and action. The international definitions and standards on human trafficking, for instance, nudged Malawi to be more proactive on combating child labor and abuse. Following the legal ban of *trokosi* in Ghana in 1998, civil society mobilized financial resources from the UN Development Fund for Women (UNIFEM) to support rescue, rehabilitation, and vocational training efforts. With financial backing, the NGO that spearheaded efforts to end the practice for years was able to continue its strategy of offering cash and material incentives to shrines in exchange for *trokosi* slaves. Today, fewer than 1,200 women and children are enslaved in Ghana, which, while tragic, constitutes a significant improvement.[18]

Legal reform, when associated with proper supportive interventions, is an essential tool that contributes to leveling the playing field for the girl child in rural Africa before she reaches adolescence.

Central to these supportive interventions is a change in attitudes and mind-set in communities and households.

7

Shifting Mind-Sets

Gathering data and evidence, as well as adopting and enforcing legal norms, can succeed in leveling the playing field only in a context of changing mind-sets. A fundamental shift in social norms related to girls and women—their value and their role—is required if girls are to be given an equal chance to flourish and become leaders. How do we shift cultural norms and practices that harm girls and women, while preserving cultural traditions and a sense of belonging and identity? How do we counter enduring superstitions and community pressures?

This mind-set starts with women and girls. Yet the view of one's potential and aspirations is shaped by families and communities. To be long-lasting and successful, interventions seeking to shift social norms must therefore include girls and women, but also boys and men. They must target households and entire communities. Encouraging girls to resist social expectations in a context where their entire social networks have not been included is otherwise unlikely to lead to long-lasting change—and could easily backfire.[1]

Where do we start? Social norms and gender identities are shaped from a very young age. This requires educating both boys and girls to value themselves and each other. It means telling them they have a right to be educated. This is what programs like Think Equal seek to achieve. Think Equal builds and delivers "an equality studies curriculum" for education ministries around the world. Targeting children from age 3, the curriculum seeks to break down gender stereotypes and build girls' self-confidence, rights awareness, and agency. In January 2017, 147 schools in 15 countries around the world started piloting the Think Equal curriculum.[2] In Malawi, my own foundation has adopted a curriculum in the schools it runs, centered on four building blocks: universal values, global understanding, service to humanity, and excellence. All children in the school are taught these values.

Role models are also powerful agents of change. They embody what is possible, and in so doing, ignite the imagination of young girls around them. The more women occupy leadership roles and, more generally, transcend restrictive identities that keep them from fulfilling their potential, the more they contribute to shifting expectations, social norms, and therefore attitudes and mind-sets. Women leaders often cite other women who broke conventions as a source of early lessons in leadership who inspired them as children.[3]

As a young girl, I used to wake up very early to go collect firewood for our family on the Zomba mountain. On the way back, my friends and I always rested under a tree opposite what was then the Parliament building, which back then was located in Zomba. One day, as I was watching MPs go into the building, I spotted a lady wearing a white hat, a black-and-white suit, and white gloves walking in. I had never seen an African woman dressed like that. "Who is she?" I asked. "That's Rose Chibambo," a passerby answered. She was the first—and at the time the only—female MP and cabinet member. And I wondered: How does a woman become an MP? How does a woman become a minister? I never forgot that woman in the white hat. Many Malawians did, however, because she was forced into exile for almost 20 years. When she came back, I was in government, and I campaigned to have a street named after her. She is mentioned in history books, not only in Malawi but at the African Union, for the role she played during the struggle for self-rule on the continent.

Creating more role models for young girls starts with the economic empowerment of women, particularly their mothers. When a woman earns an income or owns assets, she typically gains a stronger voice in her own home and in her community. She has a greater say in decisions. Her children—particularly her daughters—are likely to be better fed and better educated. And these better-educated girls, in turn, are likely to have fewer, better-educated, and healthier children.

Adolescents can also be powerful role models and agents of change for their younger siblings. I met Dorothy when she was only 12 years old and had just lost both her parents. I arranged for her to attend the Joyce Banda Foundation school. There were two conditions: she had to study hard and stay committed, and when the time came, she would give back by helping others. She was top of her class. She wanted to be a doctor, but she missed the cut by very little. She did not let this defeat her. She attended the Bunda College of Agriculture and then obtained a master's in agricultural economics at Uganda's Makerere University. This one girl has already changed the lives of several younger girls. How? She has put all her sisters through school.

Being a role model for younger girls is not limited to economics. By giving women a voice in their families and in their communities, financial independence can more easily lead to community leadership and political representation. After I left my abusive first husband, I created an association to support businesswomen. Four members of this organization, including myself, ended up standing for office and serving as MPs, ministers of gender and child welfare, and, in my case, president.

This virtuous cycle of changing the reality of girls aged 0–10 by supporting women to have a stronger voice in their homes, local communities, and countries relies on multiple pieces coming together. Economic empowerment goes hand in hand with education and access to health services and family planning. It takes deeper root when women are in positions of leadership, even at the most local level. And this, in turn, happens more readily when women are financially independent. This is why the Joyce Banda Foundation has adopted a holistic approach, addressing income generation, youth development, education, health, and leadership.

Changing mind-sets and social norms toward gender equality—including equality for young girls—must also include boys and men. This is a lesson I learned the hard way. For African women, getting—and staying—married generally provides social status and respect. Many women will choose marriage over economic independence if running a business and making money threatens that marriage. And women's economic independence can feel threatening. I remember one woman who made and sold doughnuts—until her husband intentionally mixed sand with her flour to tank her business. When I created a women's business association, my message was "This is our time." In 1992, disgruntled husbands vandalized my garment factory, which by then employed 100 people. They felt I was teaching their wives bad manners. Overnight, I lost my business—and quickly changed my tactics. I learned that change had to be handled carefully. Men must be brought along, not antagonized. The way they see their own roles must shift as well. When my husband Richard, who has been my unwavering supporter throughout our happy marriage, gently suggested to our long-serving housekeeper that perhaps he should stop beating his wife, he almost fell over in shock. "You want me to be like you?!" our housekeeper retorted, the expression on his face a mixture of shock and contempt.

Over time, I have adopted another approach: creating opportunities for women while providing them cover. In the mid-1990s, a group of women from the Lunzu area came to see me. I was still executive director of the National Association of Business Women. They had a problem. The government had provided a small lime-processing facility for the cooperative in their village. Because this village was in an area of matrilineal tradition, the land belonged to the women. Yet the men controlled the cooperative, and they controlled the income generated by the processing facility. The women wanted to be members of the cooperative, and although they kept asking, their husbands kept refusing. What should they do?

"What hurts us most, ma'am, is that we want to keep our husbands," they said. "So the choice is for us to fight with them and they leave, or to continue begging to participate. Can't you intervene?"

"I can't intervene directly," I said, "but I can help you have your own factory. And one day, you shall employ those men."

They laughed. "How can that ever be?"

They formed their own cooperative of 35 women, and with funding from the European Union, they planned to set up another small lime-processing factory and were trained to run it. They also had to open bank accounts—even if they could only sign with their thumbprint. The men in the village did not care: they had their own plant and were making money.

By the time the new facility was up and running, however, the men's factory had broken down. They turned up at the women's cooperative.

"Can we run this for you?" they asked.

The women shook their heads. "We really need your assistance," they said, "but unfortunately, our funding came with the condition that we must run this facility and the accounts ourselves."

"What about us?" the men said.

"You can still help us."

On opening day, the EU ambassador and I found the men in the village crushing stones in the mine pit. I smiled at the women, and they nodded. My prediction had become reality. Women ran the processing plant—and controlled the checkbook—while their husbands labored in the sun on their behalf.

Similarly, shifting social norms to better support young rural girls can happen only if framed in a way that highlights the benefits for everyone. If boys and men are made to lose, any progress will be short lived. For young girls, fathers are instrumental in setting expectations and values. A study in Uganda, for instance, found that male role models, particularly fathers, were key in helping girls and women transition into male-dominated industries.[4] Like many women leaders,[5] I owe much to my own father. Besides drumming into us the value of education, he also taught his daughters to stand up for themselves and not be cowed by traditional roles.

Fathers play an essential role in shaping their daughters' mind-set. Yet the typical village girl does not interact much with her father. She does not sit with him under the village *mphala*, and she hardly speaks to him. I grew up at a time when men did not cook, but my father cooked. He sat with us and talked to us. He sent us to school and made sure we studied hard. His friends laughed at him, but he didn't care. When I was a little girl, he snuck me into the State House grounds when he played for the British governor and his wife as part of the police band. We stood in the garden as the governor and his wife sat on the balcony, drinking tea. And I wondered how people came to sit on that balcony. "You see?" he told me. "You can go anywhere." Many years later, when I became president and walked into that State House, I went straight to that balcony, looked down at the garden, and wished my father was still alive. I am who I am because of my father.

Yet changes within the household—be it girls, boys, fathers, mothers, or other relatives—often require changes within communities. Mind-sets shift far more easily in a context of critical mass, rather than in isolation. And to change attitudes and behaviors within communities, Africa possesses a great asset: traditional chiefs. My own experience in Malawi has taught me that, when we properly engage the custodians of tradition, they can become effective champions of change.

In many African countries, state authority gets significantly diluted in rural and remote areas, where traditional chiefs wield at the very least significant moral, and sometimes formal, authority. An Afrobarometer survey in 36 African countries has also confirmed that local chiefs are more trusted than politicians, and traditional leaders are also perceived to be less corrupt than government officials and the police.[6] As custodians of tradition, they are well placed to shift mind-sets, attitudes, and behavior. And they are on the ground, present in every village, in touch with the local situation.

Five days after I was inaugurated as president of Malawi in 2012, I invited 350 chiefs to Mount Soche Hotel in Blantyre. "You are my fellow champions," I told them. "This nation shall be stagnant or make progress because of you and me. We must take responsibility." For the first time, traditional chiefs in Malawi were being treated as government partners in improving the well-being and empowerment of women and girls. They had a role to play besides settling local disputes and collecting money for traditional initiations. They felt valued, and they felt relevant. They became an essential part of the solution.

The first area we tackled together was maternal mortality. Through our discussions, they embraced the objective and agreed that, if more mothers, sisters, wives, and daughters had healthier pregnancies, survived childbirth, and delivered stronger babies, everybody would win. They formed a national committee, chaired by one of the senior chiefs. He was given a car, so he could travel around the country. For the first time, a man was talking about maternal health and family planning openly. He mobilized his fellow chiefs around the country; he regularly spoke on television and the radio about having fewer children, about how "real" men should look after their pregnant wives and take them to the hospital to deliver babies. In 2013, he traveled to the African Union and to the UN in New York.

Spurred by Senior Chief Kwataine, traditional leaders made their own bylaws: pregnant women should no longer deliver in villages with traditional birth attendants, but in clinics. If any woman died in childbirth in their jurisdiction, the local chiefs would be responsible. Women and birth attendants who did not comply were fined, and if a woman died in childbirth because she had not complied, the village chief also paid a fine to the traditional leader above him or her. Traditional leaders at all levels then started to compete with one another. Who would get the best result in their jurisdiction? Those who were initially skeptical noticed that other chiefs were getting results, and they began to change as well. Traditional birth attendants were also mobilized, and their role redefined as "secret mothers"—advising pregnant women and taking them to the clinic when it was time to deliver.

Traditionally, anything having to do with pregnancy was shrouded in secrecy, and women could only talk to their mother or mother-in-law about their pregnancy. Almost overnight, chiefs, husbands, traditional birth attendants, mothers, even other men in the village became the support system for pregnant women. With help from the private sector and donors, we then built shelters at the clinics—20 in 24 months—where women who traveled from remote villages ahead of their due date could stay, waiting for labor to start. Once the priorities have been articulated clearly and these traditional structures mobilized, change can happen quickly—as it did in maternal health. The same approach can be embraced in other areas critical for young girls, such as nutrition, labor, education, and harmful traditions. Encouraged by the progress on maternal health, we formed other national committees headed by chiefs to tackle nutrition and girls' education. My childhood friend Chrissie became a member of the education committee. I did not get to see the results: I was out of office before these initiatives had a chance to bear fruit. Sadly, these committees were dismantled after I left office.

Religious leaders also have a critical role to play. In some villages in southern Malawi, for instance, the church persuaded local chiefs to modify traditional initiations for girls. Local chiefs still receive payments from families, but the ceremony now happens in the church and has been stripped of the most harmful practices. Traditional healers can also be part of the solution if properly mobilized. This starts at the top, with the government deciding to engage and partner with these traditional structures—chiefs, healers, and religious leaders. Once they are on board, half the battle is won.

Engaging entire communities through partnerships among governments, civil society, traditional structures, and donors produces results. In the 1990s, I saw firsthand how USAID's Social Mobilization Campaign (SMC) in Malawi, which was initially a rather small component of the Girls' Attainment in Basic Literacy and Education Program (GABLE), successfully changed parents' and communities' attitudes toward girls' education. Person-to-person and group outreach at the grassroots level, training to sensitize teachers, and 156 weekly radio programs complemented the government's policies on secondary school scholarship and fee waivers. SMC strongly engaged with parents, community leaders, students, and education officials in identifying and modifying social attitudes and practices that constrained girls' achievement in basic education. Spanning eight years, SMC succeeded in transforming parents' attitudes toward girls and their education, which in turn increased young girls' access, persistence, and success in education. The program also led to modification of initiations, a reduction in early marriages and pregnancies, better-quality education, as well as increased involvement of local communities in their schools.[7]

One of the most successful interventions has been Tostan International's Community Empowerment Program (CEP), which has shifted attitudes toward female genital mutilation and child marriage in remote African rural villages. Between 1997 and 2015, over 7,200 rural communities in Djibouti, Gambia, Guinea, Guinea-Bissau, Mali, Mauritania, Senegal, and Somalia publicly declared they would abandon both practices following Tostan's CEP intervention. An evaluation conducted 8 to 10 years after these public declarations found that over three-quarters of these communities had indeed permanently ended the practices. The CEP interventions were also reported to have resulted in improved conflict resolution within families and communities, increased participation of women in local politics, growth in community-based civil society organizations, and better access to health services and credit.[8]

For 30 months, CEP brings together adolescents and adults of both genders in community sessions, during which they participate in discussions centered on local notions of human rights that are rooted in daily life, as well as in exercises and games that draw heavily on local cultural knowledge, especially proverbs, songs, and dances. The success of CEP has been credited to several factors: relying on social networks, and not just individuals and families, helps create a critical mass embracing change; ending harmful practices requires creating, and not just abandoning, norms; and social norms shape individual aspirations and beliefs about personal capacities.[9]

Other programs, such as CARE's interventions to mitigate the effects of child marriage in Ethiopia and Rwanda, have successfully challenged social norms to improve girls' well-being. For example, CARE has deliberately integrated social norms theory into tools and approaches in programs. Research on social norms theory has increasingly been translated into practice, and these examples demonstrate that, with carefully designed local interventions, mind-sets can be changed to support young girls.

Conclusion

So what do we do? How do we make sure that rural African girls are given a chance to fulfill their potential and become the kind of leaders that our continent so badly needs? What can we all do to make sure they are not left behind? If we are to gather the data and evidence we need, create and implement supporting legislation, and shift mind-sets so families and entire communities come to better value and support young girls, we need smart partnerships. All of us have a role to play.

African Governments
Commitment starts at the top. In a context of competing priorities and limited resources, governments' contribution is to (1) prioritize gender policies, (2) adopt a comprehensive approach that expands beyond education enrollment and health to incorporate leadership and rights, and (3) incorporate an agenda focusing on girls aged 0–10 within gender policies.

In practice:
- Actively appoint, support, and encourage competent women leaders at all levels of government. This contributes to shifting not only policy priorities but also mind-sets by creating more role models and broadening traditional gender roles.

- Mobilize and allocate resources for interventions supporting girls aged 0–10.
- Facilitate the collection of data and evidence, including on sensitive topics such as harmful traditions.
- Design and evaluate policy based on reliable data and evidence.
- Enact domestic legislation in line with international treaties and commitments related to young girls, and tackle inconsistencies within the domestic legal framework.
- Partner with civil society and traditional leaders through local government to shift mind-sets and ensure the domestication of laws.
- Adopt a school curriculum incorporating rights and leadership education for both boys and girls. Remove gender stereotypes from educational material, and include positive gender roles.

Civil Society
Supporting young girls in rural areas requires a deep knowledge of local traditions, a presence on the ground, and work with local communities. Civil society is best placed to fill that role.

In practice:

- Collect evidence focusing on girls aged 0–10 to help close the data gap. Civil society organizations rooted in local communities are well placed to collect data and evidence related to girls aged 0–10, both to identify issues and priorities and also to measure what works and what does not. Local knowledge and connections, particularly around sensitive issues, are essential to facilitate such evidence gathering.
- Inform and mobilize. What stays hidden cannot be addressed. Whoever stays isolated carries less weight. Civil society is well placed to highlight harmful practices that have not received any attention, to inform women and girls of their rights and practical recourses, or to organize support and solidarity networks for women and girls.
- Keep authorities accountable. Armed with evidence, civil society can influence policy decisions and push a gender agenda in general, and action supporting girls aged 0–10 in particular. Mobilization campaigns are effective ways to push toward action, from enacting laws to enforcing them. Such pressure was essential to the adoption of the Domestic Violence Act in Malawi, for instance, and to action against *trokosi* in Ghana.
- Work with traditional and religious authorities to provide alternatives to harmful practices and shift mind-sets.

International and Regional Organizations/Donors

Any domestic intervention, even when extending to the most rural areas, can benefit from outside support. International and regional organizations, as well as donors, can do much to support young African girls.

In practice:

- Push an international agenda specifically supporting girls aged 0–10 within gender interventions.
- Support and share best practices and training on collecting data and evidence on young girls, as well as legislation and programs that have worked elsewhere.
- Provide technical, financial, and political support to local civil society. Many African governments still consider civil society more of an adversary than a partner. I would never have been able to launch and maintain an association for businesswomen and mobilize civil society on behalf of women without support from donors. Instead, I would most likely have been arrested.
- Promote international and regional instruments and benchmarks. These promote peer pressure and competition. They also offer tools to help African governments meet their international and regional obligations by translating their commitments into domestic action.

Individuals

Change is not the prerogative of governments and organizations. Whether from Africa or elsewhere, we all have the power to make a difference for young girls.

In practice:

- Become a role model for girls. Role models inspire young girls to dream bigger and aim higher. I never forgot Rose Chibambo. I hope that being Malawi's first woman president has inspired young girls in Malawi to believe that they, too, can one day become leaders in whatever field they choose. It is never too early to become a role model. Any girl can become a role model for her siblings, her friends, and her community.
- Give back. My only request to any girl or woman I've ever helped was: persevere and help others. That way, helping just one girl ripples to several others—in the way that helping Dorothy after she'd lost both her parents later changed the lives of young girls, starting with her younger sisters. Helping one girl can indirectly change the lives of

many others. Women and girls who have been lucky enough to receive an education are in a position to help others follow in their footsteps by providing financial assistance, mentorship, or inspiration. You don't have to be in Africa to change the lives of young African girls. A number of organizations have leveraged technology so that anyone is able to directly sponsor a girl in need and establish a relationship.

- Mobilize or join existing movements. I have met extraordinary young girls in the United States who started initiatives to support their sisters in Africa. African girls and women such as Kakenya Ntayia, who underwent female genital mutilation and demanded to go to school, are speaking on the international stage to raise awareness about the plight of young girls and mobilizing for change. Kakenya has joined words and action: she is also helping other girls get the education they deserve.

We cannot afford to waste a single girl's potential. We need all our people. Africa needs all its girls. Let's get to work and pay attention to the first 10 years of life, so every girl is given a chance from day one.

Notes

Notes to Introduction

1 UNESCO, "Leaving No One Behind: How Far on the Way to Universal Primary and Secondary Education?" Policy Paper 27/Fact Sheet 37, July 2016, http://unesdoc.unesco.org/images/0024/002452/245238E.pdf.

2 Raghabendra Chattopadhyay and Esther Duflo, "Women as Policy Makers: Evidence from a Randomized Policy Experiment in India," *Econometrica* 72(5) (September 2004): 1409–1443.

3 David Dollar, Raymond Fisman, and Roberta Gatti, "Are Women Really the 'Fairer' Sex? Corruption and Women in Government," Policy Research Report on Gender and Development, Working Paper Series No. 4, World Bank, http://siteresources.worldbank.org/INTGENDER/Resources/wp4.pdf.

4 Equal Measures 2030, "Policymakers and Gender Equality: What They Know and How They Know It," September 2017, http://www.equalmeasures2030.org/wp-content/uploads/2017/09/EM-September-report-WEB.pdf.

5 World Economic Forum, *The Global Gender Gap Report 2016*, 26.

6 World Bank, "Gender and Economic Growth in Kenya, Unleashing the Power of Women," xxii, http://www.ifc.org/wps/wcm/connect/84f6b48048855d698ee4de6a6515bb18/Gender+and+Economic+Growth+in+Kenya.pdf?MOD=AJPERES.

7 Inter-Parliamentary Union, "Women in National Parliaments," http://www.ipu.org/wmn-e/classif.htm.

8 "President Kagame and AUC Chair Dr. Dlamini-Zuma Receive 'Gender Champion Award,'" July 9, 2016, http://gov.rw/news-detail/?tx_ttnews%5Btt_news%5D=1560&cHash=24f67e8008acc3fe54e5bd5fa7b09afa.

9 U.S. AID, "The United States National Action Plan on Women, Peace and Security," June 2016, 4, https://www.usaid.gov/sites/default/files/documents/1868/National%20Action%20Plan%20on%20Women%2C%20Peace%2C%20and%20Security.pdf.

10 Joyce Banda, "From Day One: An Agenda for Advancing Women Leaders in Africa," Wilson Center, March 20, 2017, https://www.wilsoncenter.org/sites/default/files/dr ._joyce_banda_from_day_one.pdf.
11 Inter-Parliamentary Union, "Women in National Parliaments."
12 Justine Uvuza, "Hidden Inequalities: Rwandan Female Politicians' Experiences of Balancing Family and Political Responsibilities," PhD dissertation, Newcastle University, 2014, https://theses.ncl.ac.uk/dspace/bitstream/10443/2475/1/Uvuza,%20J.%2014.pdf.
13 Pamela Abbott and Dixon Malunda, "The Promise and the Reality; Women's Rights in Rwanda," Oxford Human Rights Hub, University of Oxford Faculty of Law, http://ohrh .law.ox.ac.uk/wordpress/wp-content/uploads/2014/04/OxHRH-Working-Paper -Series-No-5-Abott-and-Malunda.pdf.
14 World Bank, "World Bank Group to Invest $2.5 Billion in Education Projects Benefit- ing Adolescent Girls," press release, April 13, 2016, http://www.worldbank.org/en/news /press-release/2016/04/13/world-bank-group-to-invest-25-billion-in-education -projects-benefiting-adolescent-girls.
15 Coalition for Adolescent Girls, "Why Girls?" http://coalitionforadolescentgirls.org /about-us/why-girls/.

Notes to Chapter 1

 1 FAO, "Gender and Nutrition," http://www.fao.org/docrep/012/al184e/al184e00.pdf.
 2 Bridge, "Gender and Food Security: Towards Gender-Just Food and Nutrition Security," Overview Report 2014, 22–23, https://opendocs.ids.ac.uk/opendocs/bitstream/handle /123456789/5245/IDS_Bridge_Food_Security_Report_Online.pdf?sequence=3.
 3 Robert E. Black et al., "Maternal and Child Undernutrition and Overweight in Low- Income and Middle-Income Countries," *The Lancet* 382(9890) (August 3, 2013): 427–451, http://www.thelancet.com/journals/lancet/article/PIIS0140-6736%2813%2960937-X /abstract.
 4 WHO/UNICEF/World Bank Group, "Levels and Trends in Child Malnutrition," Joint Child Malnutrition Estimates, Key Findings of the 2017 Edition, http://www.who.int /nutgrowthdb/jme_brochoure2017.pdf?ua=1.
 5 World Bank, "The World Bank and Nutrition, Overview," http://www.worldbank.org /en/topic/nutrition/overview.
 6 World Bank, "The World Bank and Nutrition, Overview."
 7 "Global Hunger Index, Africa Edition 2016," http://ebrary.ifpri.org/utils/getfile/collection /p15738coll2/id/131131/filename/131342.pdf.
 8 FAO, "The State of Food and Agriculture 2010–11," 125.
 9 UNICEF, "Gender Action Plan 2014–2017," 14, https://www.unicef.org/gender/files /UNICEF_Gender_Action_Plan_2014-2017.pdf.
10 FAO, "Gender and Nutrition."
11 FAO, "The State of Food and Agriculture 2010–11," 125.
12 FAO, "The State of Food and Agriculture 2010–11," 125.
13 World Bank, "World Development Report 2012," 88.
14 World Bank, http://www.worldbank.org/en/topic/health/publication/nutrition-country -profiles.
15 World Bank, "World Development Report 2012," 87–88.
16 FAO, "The State of Food and Agriculture 2010–11," 125.
17 World Bank, "Nutrition at a Glance—Malawi."
18 World Bank, "The World Bank and Nutrition, Overview."

19 Black et al., "Maternal and Child Undernutrition and Overweight."

20 FAO, "The State of Food and Agriculture 2010–11," 111–112.

21 World Bank and ONE Campaign, "Levelling the Field: Improving Opportunities for Women Farmers in Africa," March 2014, http://documents.worldbank.org/curated/en /579161468007198488/Levelling-the-field-improving-opportunities-for-women -farmers-in-Africa.

22 World Bank, "World Development Report 2012," 83.

23 FAO, "The State of Food and Agriculture 2010–11," 111–112, 118–119.

24 World Bank and ONE Campaign, "Levelling the Field."

25 FAO, "The State of Food and Agriculture 2010–11."

26 FAO, "The State of Food and Agriculture 2010–11."

27 Robert Gilbert, Webster Sakala, and Todd Benson, "Gender Analysis of a Nationwide Cropping System Trial Survey in Malawi," *African Studies Quarterly* 6 (2002), https:// asq.africa.ufl.edu/gilbert_sakala_benson_spring02/.

28 Christopher Udry, "Gender, Agricultural Production, and the Theory of the Household," *Journal of Political Economy* 104(5) (October 1996): 1010–1046.

29 Gautam Hazarika and Basudeb Guha-Khasnobis, "Household Access to Microcredit and Children's Food Security in Rural Malawi: A Gender Perspective," Discussion Paper 3793, Institute for the Study of Labor (IZA), 2008, https://papers.ssrn.com/sol3/papers .cfm?abstract_id=1293585##.

30 FAO, "Gender and Nutrition."

Notes to Chapter 2

1 UNICEF, "Harnessing the Power of Data for Girls: Taking Stock and Looking Ahead to 2030," October 2016, https://data.unicef.org/wp-content/uploads/2016/10/Harnessing -the-Power-of-Data-for-Girls-Brochure-2016-1-1.pdf.

2 UNICEF, "Harnessing the Power of Data for Girls."

3 Plan International, "Tackling Child Labor on Malawi's Tobacco Farms," June 6, 2011, https://plan-international.org/blog/2015/05/tackling-child-labour-malawis-tobacco -farms#.

4 International Labour Organization, "Children in Hazardous Work: What We Know, What We Need to Do," International Programme for the Elimination of Child Labour, 2011, 21–25.

5 Albertine de Lange, "Gender Dimensions of Rural Child Labour in Africa," 2009, http://www.fao-ilo.org/fileadmin/user_upload/fao_ilo/pdf/Papers/17_March /Delange_final.doc_12_may.pdf.

6 "Malawi: 2015 National Child Labour Survey Report," 72 (Table A3), http://www.ilo .org/ipec/Informationresources/WCMS_IPEC_PUB_29055/lang—en/index.htm.

7 International Labour Office, "Global Estimates of Child Labour: Results and Trends, 2012–2016," 2017, http://www.ilo.org/wcmsp5/groups/public/@dgreports/@dcomm /documents/publication/wcms_575499.pdf.

8 International Labour Organization, "Children in Hazardous Work," 28–29.

9 International Labour Organization, "Child Domestic Work: Global Estimates 2012," International Programme for the Elimination of Child Labour, http://www.ilo.org/ipec /Informationresources/WCMS_IPEC_PUB_23235/lang—en/index.htm.

10 International Labour Organization, "Child Domestic Work: Global Estimates 2012."

11 International Labour Office, "Global Estimates of Child Labour."

12 World Bank, "Gender, Time Use and Poverty in Sub-Saharan Africa," World Bank Working Paper 73, 2006, http://siteresources.worldbank.org/INTAFRREGTOPGENDER /Resources/gender_time_use_pov.pdf.

13 World Bank, "Gender, Time Use and Poverty in Sub-Saharan Africa."

14 "Malawi: 2015 National Child Labour Survey Report," 69–70 (Table A1), http://www .ilo.org/ipec/Informationresources/WCMS_IPEC_PUB_29055/lang—en/index.htm.

15 UNICEF, "Harnessing the Power of Data for Girls."

16 International Labour Office, "Global Estimates of Child Labour."

17 World Bank, "Gender, Time Use and Poverty in Sub-Saharan Africa."

18 International Labour Organization, "Gender and Child Labour in Agriculture," http:// www.ilo.org/ipec/areas/Agriculture/WCMS_172261/lang—en/index.htm; "Harnessing the Power of Data for Girls."

19 International Labour Organization, "Children in Hazardous Work," 28–29.

20 International Labour Organization, "Children in Hazardous Work," 21–25.

21 Plan International, "Tackling Child Labor on Malawi's Tobacco Farms."

Notes to Chapter 3

1 East Central and Southern African Health Community, "Child Sexual Abuse in Sub-Saharan Africa: A Review of the Literature," January 2011, 15, http://www.svri.org/sites /default/files/attachments/2016-07-16/Draft%20Child%20Sexual%20Abuse%20In%20 Sub-Saharan%20Africa%20A%20Review%20Of%20The%20Literature.pdf.

2 UNICEF, "Hidden in Plain Sight: A Statistical Analysis of Violence against Children—Summary," https://www.unicef.org/publications/files/Hidden_in_plain _sight_statistical_analysis_Summary_EN_2_Sept_2014.pdf.

3 UNICEF Eastern and Southern Africa, "Gender and Education," https://www.unicef .org/esaro/7310_Gender_and_education.html.

4 East Central and Southern African Health Community, "Child Sexual Abuse in Sub-Saharan Africa," 14.

5 WHO, UNODC, and UNDP, "Global Status Report on Violence Prevention 2014," 14–15, http://www.who.int/violence_injury_prevention/violence/status_report/2014/en/.

6 East Central and Southern African Health Community, "Child Sexual Abuse in Sub-Saharan Africa," 14, 21.

7 UNICEF, "Child Marriage Is a Violation of Human Rights but Is All Too Common," http://data.unicef.org/topic/child-protection/child-marriage/#.

8 UNICEF, "Hidden in Plain Sight," 4.

9 East Central and Southern African Health Community, "Child Sexual Abuse in Sub-Saharan Africa," 14.

10 UNICEF data, http://data.unicef.org/topic/child-protection/female-genital-mutilation -and-cutting/.

11 UNICEF, "UNICEF's Data Work on FMG/C," UNICEF, https://www.unicef.org/media /files/FGMC_2016_brochure_final_UNICEF_SPREAD.pdf.

12 U.S. Department of State, Bureau of Democracy, Human Rights and Labor, "Malawi 2016 Human Rights Report," 16, https://www.state.gov/documents/organization /265486.pdf.

13 UNICEF, "Hidden in Plain Sight," 5.

14 World Health Organization, "Global and Regional Estimates of Violence against Women: Prevalence and Health Effects of Intimate Partner Violence and Non-Partner

Sexual Violence," 2013, 20 (Table 5), http://apps.who.int/iris/bitstream/10665/85239/1/9789241564625_eng.pdf?ua=1.

15 East Central and Southern African Health Community, "Child Sexual Abuse in Sub-Saharan Africa," 19.

16 Ed Butler, "The Man Hired to Have Sex with Children," BBC News, July 21, 2016, http://www.bbc.com/news/magazine-36843769.

17 BBC News, "Malawi 'Hyena Man' Eric Aniva Sentenced to Two Years Hard Labor," November 22, 2016, http://www.bbc.com/news/world-africa-38063345.

Notes to Chapter 4

1 World Bank, "World Development Indicators."

2 Equal Measures 2030, "Policy Makers and Gender Equality: What They Know and How They Know It," 12, http://www.equalmeasures2030.org/wp-content/uploads/2017/09/EM-September-report-WEB.pdf.

3 UNESCO, "Leaving No One Behind: How Far on the Way to Universal Primary and Secondary Education?" Policy Paper 27/Fact Sheet 37, July 3, 2016, http://unesdoc.unesco.org/images/0024/002452/245238E.pdf.

4 UNESCO, "Leaving No One Behind," 6.

5 UNESCO, "Global Education Monitoring Report," interactive database, http://www.education-inequalities.org/indicators/edu_out_pry#?sort=mean&dimension=sex&group=all&age_group=edu_out_pry&countries=.

6 UNESCO, "Global Education Monitoring Report."

7 World Bank, "World Development Report 2012: Gender Equality and Development," 2, https://siteresources.worldbank.org/INTWDR2012/Resources/7778105-1299699968583/7786210-1315936222006/Complete-Report.pdf.

8 National Statistical Office of Malawi, "Malawi: 2015–2016 Demographic and Health Survey, Key Findings," 3, https://dhsprogram.com/pubs/pdf/SR237/SR237.pdf.

9 Theresa Tuwor and Marie-Antoinette Sossou, "Gender Discrimination and Education in West Africa: Strategies for Maintaining Girls in School," *International Journal of Inclusive Education* 12(4) (2008): 363–379, http://www.tandfonline.com/doi/full/10.1080/13603110601183115?scroll=top&needAccess=true.

10 Cynthia B. Lloyd and Ann K. Blanc, "Children's Schooling in Sub-Saharan Africa: The Role of Fathers, Mothers, and Others," *Population and Development Review* 22(2) (June 1996): 265–298.

11 UNESCO, "Regional Overview: Sub-Saharan Africa," 5, http://en.unesco.org/gem-report/sites/gem-report/files/157229E.pdf.

12 UNESCO, "Leaving No One Behind," 5, 8.

13 UNESCO, "Leaving No One Behind," 7.

14 UNICEF, "Malawi—The Situation of Women and Children," https://www.unicef.org/malawi/children.html.

15 World Bank, "Globally, Periods Are Causing Girls to Be Absent from School," June 2016, http://blogs.worldbank.org/education/globally-periods-are-causing-girls-be-absent-school.

16 Lloyd and Blanc, "Children's Schooling in Sub-Saharan Africa."

17 Sharmilla Ganesan, "What Do Women Leaders Have in Common?" *The Atlantic*, August 17, 2016, https://www.theatlantic.com/business/archive/2016/08/what-do-women-leaders-have-in-common/492656/.

18   UNESCO, "Regional Overview: Sub-Saharan Africa."

19   Francisco Campos, Markus Goldstein, Laura McGorman, Ana Maria Munoz Boudet, and Obert Pimhidzai, "Breaking the Metal Ceiling: Female Entrepreneurs Who Succeed in Male-Dominated Sectors," Policy Research Working Paper 7503, World Bank, December 2015.

20   Cynthia B. Lloyd and Barbara S. Mensch, "Marriage and Childbirth as Factors in Dropping Out from School: An Analysis of DHS Data from Sub-Saharan Africa," *Population Studies: A Journal of Demography* 62(1) (2008): 1–13.

21   Tuwor and Soussou, "Gender Discrimination and Education in West Africa."

22   UNESCO, "Regional Overview: Sub-Saharan Africa," 6.

23   UNESCO, "The Impact of Women Teachers on Girls' Education," 2006, 1–2, http://unesdoc.unesco.org/images/0014/001459/145990e.pdf.

24   Lloyd and Blanc, "Children's Schooling in Sub-Saharan Africa."

25   UNESCO, "Leaving No One Behind," 13.

Notes to Chapter 5

1   Mayra Buvinic and Eric Swanson, "Where Are the Gender Data? Three Steps to Better Data and Closing Gaps," Center for Global Development, September 18, 2017, https://www.cgdev.org/blog/where-are-gender-data-three-steps-better-data-closing-gaps.

2   http://www.oecd.org/dac/gender-development/thedacgenderequalitypolicymarker.htm.

3   Open Data Watch and Gender2X, "Ready to Measure Phase II: Indicators Available to Monitor SGD Gender Targets," http://www.data2x.org/wp-content/uploads/2017/09/Ready-to-Measure-Phase-II_Report.pdf.

4   *New York Times*, "Closing the Gender Data Gap," paid for and posted by the Bill and Melinda Gates Foundation, https://paidpost.nytimes.com/gates-foundation/closing-the-gender-data-gap.html.

5   Population Council, "Building Girls' Protective Assets: A Collection of Tools for Program Design," http://www.popcouncil.org/uploads/pdfs/2016PGY_GirlsProtectiveAssetsTools.pdf.

6   *New York Times*, "Closing the Gender Data Gap."

7   https://www.younglives.org.uk.

8   http://techmousso.ci.

9   Kelli Rogers, "When Gender Data Became Cool," Devex, August 2, 2016, https://www.devex.com/news/when-gender-data-became-cool-88548.

10   *New York Times*, "Closing the Gender Data Gap."

11   Save the Children, "Young Voices Want to Be Heard," https://resourcecentre.savethechildren.net/story/young-voices-want-be-heard.

12   https://www.younglives.org.uk/node/8039.

13   Save the Children, "Young Voices Want to be Heard."

14   Save the Children, "Young Voices Want to be Heard."

15   UNICEF's Office of Research, Innocenti, the Childwatch International Research Network, the Centre for Children and Young People at Southern Cross University, Australia, and the Children's Issues Centre at the University of Otago, New Zealand.

16   http://childethics.com.

17   Malawi Human Rights Commission, "A Study into Cultural Practices and Their Impact on the Enjoyment of Human Rights, Particularly the Rights of Women and Children in Malawi," May 2006, 8, https://www.eldis.org/document/A56280.

18 Data2X, "Mapping Gender Data Gaps," March 2014, http://www.data2x.org/wp -content/uploads/2017/11/Data2X_MappingGenderDataGaps_ExecutiveSummary .pdf.

19 Data2X, "Working Brief: Data for Adolescent Girls," http://www.data2x.org/wp -content/uploads/2016/10/Data2X-Adolescent-Girls-Data-Brief.pdf.

20 UN Woman, "Flagship Programme: Making Every Woman and Girl Count," http:// www.unwomen.org/en/how-we-work/flagship-programmes/making-every-woman -and-girl-count.

21 Rogers, "When Gender Data Became Cool."

22 http://whatworks.co.za.

23 https://www.idrc.ca/en/initiative/growth-and-economic-opportunities-women.

24 http://www.worldbank.org/en/programs/africa-gender-innovation-lab.

25 Equal Measures 2030, "Policymakers and Gender Equality: What They Know and How They Know It," September 2017, 4, http://www.equalmeasures2030.org/wp-content /uploads/2017/09/EM-September-report-WEB.pdf.

26 Equal Measures 2030, "Policymakers and Gender Equality," 4; Sophie Edwards, "Policy-makers Flying Blind on Gender Issues, Survey Finds," Devex, September 20, 2017, https://www.devex.com/news/policymakers-flying-blind-on-gender-issues-survey -finds-91071.

27 http://www.equalmeasures2030.org.

Notes to Chapter 6

1 Ben Crisman, Sarah Dykstra, Charles Kenny, and Megan O'Donnell, "The Impact of Legislation on the Hazard of Female Genital Mutilation: Regression Discontinuity Evidence from Burkina Faso," Working Paper 432, Center for Global Development, July 2016, https://www.cgdev.org/sites/default/files/impact-legislation-hazard-female -genital-mutilationcutting-regression-discontinuity.pdf.

2 Joyce Banda and Priscilla Atansah, "An Agenda for Harmful Cultural Practices and Girls' Empowerment," Center for Global Development, December 12, 2016, https://www .cgdev.org/publication/agenda-harmful-cultural-practices-and-girls-empowerment.

3 U.S. Department of Labor, Bureau of International Labor Affairs, "Child Labor and Forced Labor Reports, Malawi," https://www.dol.gov/agencies/ilab/resources/reports /child-labor/malawi.

4 Banda and Atansah, "An Agenda for Harmful Cultural Practices and Girls' Empowerment."

5 World Bank and IFC, "Women, Business and the Law 2014," 33, http://wbl.worldbank .org/~/media/WBG/WBL/Documents/Reports/2014/Women-Business-and-the-Law -2014-FullReport.pdf?la=en.

6 World Bank, "Women, Business and the Law," online database, http://wbl.worldbank .org.

7 Matt Collin and Theodore Talbot, "Does Banning Child Marriage Really Work?" Center for Global Development, August 22, 2014, https://www.cgdev.org/blog/does -banning-child-marriage-really-work.

8 Banda and Atansah, "An Agenda for Harmful Cultural Practices and Girls' Empowerment."

9 "Malawi 2016 Human Rights Report," 15.

10 Crisman, Dykstra, Kenny, and O'Donnell, "The Impact of Legislation on the Hazard of Female Genital Mutilation," 31.

11 "Malawi 2016 Human Rights Report," 15.
12 "Malawi 2016 Human Rights Report," 18.
13 http://www.popcouncil.org/news/the-girl-roster-an-innovative-approach-to-ending-the-gender-data-gap.
14 Nina Buchmann, Erica Field, Rachel Glennerster, Shahana Nazneen, Svetlana Pimkina, and Iman Sen, "Power vs Money: Alternative Approaches to Reducing Child Marriage in Bangladesh, a Randomized Control Trial," May 12, 2017, https://www.povertyactionlab.org/sites/default/files/publications/100_child-marriage-bangladesh-May2017.pdf.
15 International Center for Research on Women, "New Insights on Preventing Child Marriage: A Global Analysis of Factors and Programs," 39, https://www.icrw.org/wp-content/uploads/2016/10/New-Insights-on-Preventing-Child-Marriage.pdf; David McKenzie, "School Pays Dowry to Save Girls from Childhood Marriage," CNN, June 16, 2011, http://www.cnn.com/2011/WORLD/africa/06/16/kenya.school.maasai/index.html.
16 Banda and Atansah, "An Agenda for Harmful Cultural Practices and Girls' Empowerment."
17 Banda and Atansah, "An Agenda for Harmful Cultural Practices and Girls' Empowerment."
18 Banda and Atansah, "An Agenda for Harmful Cultural Practices and Girls' Empowerment."

Notes to Chapter 7

1 Bapu Vaitla, Alice Taylor, Julia Van Horn, and Ben Cislaghi, "Social Norms and Girls' Well-Being: Linking Theory and Practice," Data2X, July 2017, 5, http://www.data2x.org/wp-content/uploads/2017/07/Social-Norms.pdf.
2 http://www.thinkequal.com.
3 Sharmilla Ganesan, "What Do Women Leaders Have in Common?" *The Atlantic*, August 17, 2016, https://www.theatlantic.com/business/archive/2016/08/what-do-women-leaders-have-in-common/492656/.
4 Francisco Campos, Markus Goldstein, Laura McGorman, Ana Maria Munoz Boudet, and Obert Pimhidzai, "Breaking the Metal Ceiling: Female Entrepreneurs Who Succeed in Male-Dominated Sectors," Policy Research Working Paper 7503, World Bank, December 2015.
5 Ganesan, "What Do Women Leaders Have in Common?"
6 *The Economist*, "Africa's Chiefs Are More Trusted Than Its Politicians," December 19, 2017, https://www.economist.com/news/middle-east-and-africa/21732852-traditional-leaders-have-little-formal-power-so-they-have-earn-trust-africas.
7 The Mitchell Group, "Summative Evaluation of USAID/Malawi's Girls' Attainment in Basic Literacy and Education," May 30, 2002, 18–23, http://pdf.usaid.gov/pdf_docs/Pdabw640.pdf.
8 Vaitla et al., "Social Norms and Girls' Well-Being," 13.
9 Vaitla et al., "Social Norms and Girls' Well-Being," 15–16.

About the Authors

Joyce Banda served as the President of the Republic of Malawi from 2012–2014. She was Malawi's first female president and Africa's second. Prior to assuming office, President Banda served as a Member of Parliament, Minister of Gender and Child Welfare, Foreign Minister, and Vice President of the Republic of Malawi. While serving as Minister of Gender and Child Welfare, she championed the enactment of the Prevention of Domestic Violence Bill (2006), which provided the legal framework to support the prevention and elimination of all forms of violence against women and girls. President Banda is a former Distinguished Visiting Fellow at the Center for Global Development.

Caroline Lambert is an award-winning former journalist and former visiting fellow at the Center for Global Development. While a staff journalist for *The Economist*, Lambert won several awards for her coverage of Southern Africa's politics and business from Johannesburg. She also reported on conflict and post-conflict situations in Algeria, Afghanistan, Liberia, Sierra Leone, and Zimbabwe. Before becoming a journalist, she worked for the World Bank. She is the coauthor of *Oil to Cash: Fighting the Resource Curse through Cash Transfers* (Center for Global Development, 2015).

The Center for Global Development works to reduce global poverty and improve lives through innovative economic research that drives better policy and practice by the world's top decision makers.

We generate new ideas, actionable policy proposals and independent research, and spark critical global development conversations.

We focus on the intersection of developing countries and the governments, institutions and corporations that can help them deliver the greatest progress.

Our scholars conduct rigorous, impartial analysis, informed by evidence and experts from around the world.